Lecture Notes in Artificial Intelligence 11463

Subseries of Lecture Notes in Computer Science

More information about this series at http://www.springer.com/series/1244

Paul Davidsson · Harko Verhagen (Eds.)

Multi-Agent-Based Simulation XIX

19th International Workshop, MABS 2018
Stockholm, Sweden, July 14, 2018
Revised Selected Papers

Editors
Paul Davidsson
Malmö University
Malmö, Sweden

Harko Verhagen
Stockholm University
Kista, Sweden

ISSN 0302-9743   ISSN 1611-3349   (electronic)
Lecture Notes in Artificial Intelligence
ISBN 978-3-030-22269-7   ISBN 978-3-030-22270-3   (eBook)
https://doi.org/10.1007/978-3-030-22270-3

LNCS Sublibrary: SL7 – Artificial Intelligence

This Springer imprint is published by the registered company Springer Nature Switzerland AG
The registered company address is: Gewerbestrasse 11, 6330 Cham, Switzerland

Preface

The Multi-Agent-Based Simulation (MABS) Workshop series aims to bring together researchers interested in MAS engineering with researchers focused on finding efficient solutions to model complex social systems, in such areas as economics, management, organizational and social sciences in general. In all these areas, agent theories, metaphors, models, analysis, experimental designs, empirical studies, and methodological principles, all converge into simulation as a way of achieving explanations and predictions, exploration and testing of hypotheses, better designs and systems.

The 2018 International Multi-Agent-Based Simulation Workshop was part of the Federated AI Meeting (FAIM) that took place in Stockholm, July 14, 2018. It included the 17th International Conference on Autonomous Agents and Multiagent Systems (AAMAS), the 35th International Conference on Machine Learning (ICML), the 27th International Joint Conference on Artificial Intelligence (IJCAI), and the 23rd European Conference on Artificial Intelligence (ECAI).

This volume represents the 19th in a series that began in 1998. In total, 15 papers were submitted to the workshop. We selected ten papers for presentation through peer-review (single blind and three reviewers per paper), and invited two keynote presentations, of which one resulted in a paper included in these proceedings. The papers presented at the workshop were extended and revised, incorporating points from the discussions held at the workshop as well as from a second round of peer-review, resulting in 11 papers.

The workshop could not have taken place without the contribution of many people. We are very grateful to our keynote speakers Koen H. Van Dam (Imperial Collage, London) and Bruce Edmonds (Manchester Metropolitan University), as well as to all the MABS 2018 participants who took part in a lively debate during the presentation of the papers. We are also very grateful to all the members of the Program Committee for their hard work. Thanks are also due to Catholijn Jonker and Gal Kaminka (AAMAS 2018 workshop chairs), to Elisabeth Andre and Sven Koenig (AAMAS 2018 general co-chairs), and to Franziska Klügl (AAMAS 2018 local arrangements chair).

March 2019

Paul Davidsson
Harko Verhagen

Organization

Chairs

Paul Davidsson   Malmö University, Sweden
Harko Verhagen   Stockholm University, Sweden

Steering Committee

Frédéric Amblard   Toulouse 1 Capitole University, France
Luis Antunes   University of Lisbon, Portugal
Paul Davidsson   Malmö University, Sweden
Nigel Gilbert   University of Surrey, UK
Tim Gulden   George Mason University, USA
Emma Norling   Manchester Metropolitan University, UK
Mario Paolucci   National Research Council, Italy
Jaime Simão Sichman   University of São Paulo, Brazil
Takao Terano   Tokyo Institute of Technology, Japan

Program Committee

Diana Adamatti   Federal University of Rio Grande, Brazil
Frederic Amblard   Toulouse 1 Capitole University, France
Luis Antunes   University of Lisbon, Portugal
Joao Balsa   University of Lisbon, Portugal
Federico Bianchi   University of Bresica, Italy
Tibor Bosse   Vrije Universiteit in Amsterdam, The Netherlands
Cristiano Castelfranchi   ISTC-CNR, Italy
Sung-Bae Cho   Yonsei University, South Korea
Helder Coelho   University of Lisbon, Portugal
Frank Dignum   Utrecht University, The Netherlands
Virginia Dignum   Umeå University, Sweden
Graçaliz P. Dimuro   Federal University of Rio Grande, Brazil
Bruce Edmonds   Manchester Metropolitan University, UK
Nigel Gilbert   University of Surrey, UK
William Griffin   Arizona State University, USA
Laszlo Gulyas   AITIA International Informatics Inc.
Rainer Hegselmann   University of Bayreuth, Germany
Marco Janssen   Arizona State University, USA
William Kennedy   George Mason University, USA
Ruth Meyer   Manchester Metropolitan University, UK
John Murphy   Argonne National Laboratory, USA
Jean-Pierre Muller   CIRAD, France

Luis Gustavo Nardin	Brandenburg University of Technology, Germany
Paulo Novais	University of Minho, Portugal
Emma Norling	University of Sheffield, UK
Juan Pavón	Complutense University of Madrid, Spain
Mario Paolucci	ISTC-CNR, Italy
Gary Polhill	James Hutton Institute, UK
William Rand	University of Maryland, USA
Juliette Rouchier	Greqam/CNRS, France
Jaime Sichman	University of Sao Paulo, Brazil
Klaus Troitzsch	University of Koblenz, Germany
Natalie Van Der Wal	Vrije University Amsterdam, The Netherlands

Additional Reviewers

| Daniel Formolo | Vrije University Amsterdam, The Netherlands |
| Lenin Medeiros | Vrije University Amsterdam, The Netherlands |

Contents

Using Agent-Based Modelling to Inform Policy – What Could *Possibly* Go Wrong?

Bruce Edmonds[✉] and Lia ní Aodha

Centre for Policy Modelling, Manchester Metropolitan University,
Manchester, UK
bruce@edmonds.name
http://cfpm.org

Abstract. Scientific modelling can make things *worse*, as in the case of the North Atlantic Cod Fisheries Collapse. Some of these failures have been attributed to the simplicity of the models used compared to what they are trying to model. MultiAgent-Based Simulation (MABS) pushes the boundaries of what can be simulated, prompting many to assume that it can usefully inform policy, even in the face of complexity. That said, MABS also brings with it new difficulties and potential confusions. This paper surveys some of the pitfalls that can arise when MABS analysts try to do this. Researchers who claim (or imply) that MABS can reliably predict are criticised in particular. However, an alternative is suggested – that of using MABS for a kind of uncertainty analysis – identifying some of the possible ways a policy can go wrong (or indeed go right). A fisheries example is given. This alternative may widen, rather than narrow, the range of evidence and possibilities that are considered, which could enrich the policy-making process. We call this *Reflexive Possibilistic Modelling*.

> *"Naturally, politicians will look for any information or argument they can find to advance their agendas-that is their job"* [1, p. 83].

1 Introduction – The Cautionary Example of the North Atlantic Cod Fisheries Collapse

On the 2nd July 1992 Canada's fisheries minister, John Crosbie, placed a moratorium on all cod fishing off the northeast coast of Newfoundland and Labrador. That day 30,000 people lost their jobs and hundreds of years fishing for cod off those coasts ended. The cod were declared commercially extinct [2]. Much research has been done seeking to explain the collapse, and many answers have been put forth – ranging from simplified narratives of overfishing, to environmental conditions, and poor management. A number of authors, however, have looked at the role played by fisheries science, arguing it and its models played a pivotal role in this collapse [2, 3].

Tracing the development of this fishery, and its management, the work of these scholars has recounted how, as the fishery was developed, both fisheries science and the policies it informed became increasingly centred on counting how many fish were in the sea [4] and predicting how many could be caught, with both of these processes

© Springer Nature Switzerland AG 2019
P. Davidsson and H. Verhagen (Eds.): MABS 2018, LNAI 11463, pp. 1–16, 2019.
https://doi.org/10.1007/978-3-030-22270-3_1

feeding back on one another [2, 3, 5]. This, in turn, resulted in the development of increasingly intricate mathematical models which—partly due to the traditions in the field and the complex data they were trying to fit—became ever more divorced from reality [3, 5].

A series of scientific blunders (based on models) were made in the years leading up to the moratorium, in spite of repeated concerns being raised by inshore fishermen [3]. For example, a number of Commissions investigating the status of the cod, at the behest of the fishermen's concerns, failed to made adequate inferences about the ailing stock health. The findings of these Commissions were buoyed by model-based assessments that depicted an increasing (rather than diminishing) resource base. These predictions saw development and investment in the fishery continue throughout much of the 1980s. During this time these figures were consistently challenged by inshore fishermen [3].

It was not until 1989 that what turned out to be an erroneous forecasting of fish stocks was corrected. The fisheries department issued its annual assessment based upon revised mathematical models, which indicated that abundance had been overestimated by as much as a factor of two [3]. The subsequent Harris Commission found that the fisheries department's estimates of stock strength were based upon data, methodologies, and models of such poor quality as to be essentially useless as a 'rational' basis for management or commercial planning. The executive summary of the Harris Report [6, p. 2] states that:

> "...scientists, lulled by false data signals and, to some extent, overconfident of the validity of their predictions, failed to recognize the statistical inadequacies in their bulk biomass model and failed to properly acknowledge and recognize the high risk involved with state-of-stock advice based on relatively short and unreliable data series. Furthermore, the Panel is concerned that weaknesses in scientific management and the peer review process permitted this to happen."

Finlayson [3, pp. 12–15] argues that part of what had occurred was that scientists and policymakers had become so committed to their particular description of reality, and the idea of a strongly rebuilding stock, that this reality was read back into the scientific models.

Thus scientific models *can* make things worse – especially in cases where the modelling has been co-opted as part of the policy-making process! If this is true of the relatively simple but technical models that were being applied to questions of fisheries management in the 90's, how much more might this be true of the complex yet persuasive agent-based models now? This paper reviews some of the pitfalls of using multiagent-based simulation (MABS) within the policy domain and ends by suggesting a positive way such simulations could be used, in a manner that may widen, rather than narrow, the range of evidence and possibilities that are taken into consideration.

2 Some Pitfalls in Using Agent-Based Modelling for Policy

There are a number of confusions and mistakes that can occur when analysts and policy actors interact. This is not very surprising because these roles come with very different sets of: skills, terminology, issues, assumptions and goals. Here we briefly discuss some of the pitfalls that may arise, from the point of view of a MABS analyst. We do not concentrate on those that are obvious to modellers, such as testing and checking your model thoroughly, but focus more on the pitfalls modellers may not have thought of. A fuller discussion of these may be found here [7].

Institutionalised Assumptions

All models, including complex models, contain assumptions about reality [1]. Oftentimes we make these choices without even realising it. These assumptions may be related to the theories we use, the fields we engage in, or wider cultural biases [8]. Whilst some may be based on empirical evidence, others might be wholly unverified [9]. They may, for example, be based on disciplinary theories that have never been proved beyond theory. Though we might not always be aware of these assumptions, together they will determine what goes into a model and what does not [10]. The danger here arises when erroneous assumptions that bear little or no resemblance to reality become institutionalised orthodoxies [11]. Models from neoclassical economics and the untested models of human agency and behaviour embedded within these [12] are good examples of this. However, it has been argued that more complex simulation models are guilty of this also [13]. A good way to circumvent this problem is to be as explicit with ourselves (and others) about the assumptions we are making about reality, including those which may be taken-for-granted within (and often beyond) our fields, and be as comprehensive as possible.

Theoretical Spectacles

Though we may not often acknowledge it, oftentimes our disciplinary biases [14], will likely entail a commitment to a worldview that leans towards some value system over others, or depicting aspects of that worldview over others in a model. Thomas Kuhn described this effect as wearing 'theoretical spectacles' [15]—the theories one believes leads one to only notice the aspects of the world that fit those theories. Empirical studies have suggested that when analysts spend much of their time producing and studying simulations rather than less mediated empirical representations (such as new kinds of evidence), critical distance becomes difficult to maintain [16]. Consequently, the danger of 'theoretical spectacles' is particularly acute for modellers, and can lead modellers to see the world 'through' their models, developing a strong confirmation bias [10]. The danger here is mistaking a model- or theory-driven view for reality, and hence failing to even consider alternatives. This becomes especially important in the policy-making process, as theory choices (and their underlying normative basis) can end up driving policy choices, with different theories likely implying very different policy prescriptions, often with quite diverging social visions and practical implications [17].

Model Spread

One advantage of formal models is that they can be copied and used extensively with little effort. This is advantageous in the sense that it allows others to inspect, critique, and improve these models. It is disadvantageous, however, in the sense that once accepted, models tend to proliferate and spread uncritically. The ease of their re-use means that it can be tempting to reuse them, without retesting them, or evaluating their applicability to the task at hand. The danger here is that once a model becomes widespread others (both scientists and policymakers) then take this as a mark of its quality so it spreads even more. In an academic setting, this may not be too serious. However, in a policy setting the institutional acceptance of a poor model can have deleterious effects, with models working to concretise assumptions that though incorrect, may have moral weight [17]. Awareness of this pitfall is especially pertinent given studies have indicated that undue confidence can rise with distance from the site of knowledge production [16, 18].

Confusions over Model Purpose

Good models will have or should have, a clearly stated purpose. Such a model should have been designed with that purpose in mind and tested with respect to this. When published, its quality will have been judged against that purpose [19]. Models are not (or are almost never) general-purpose tools but more specific encapsulations of knowledge that have a quite specific scope of use. In many cases, if one does not know whether a model is being used beyond its scope, then it might be better to simply not use it at all—sometimes it is better to know the limitations of one's knowledge than to think one has some idea (or baseline) of what is happening.

Not Knowing Model Limitations

Sometimes it is easy to forget the provisional relationship between our models and reality (18). It has been suggested elsewhere that this danger may be particularly acute with complex simulation models, on account of the impression of verisimilitude that they give [16, 20]. All models however, have limitations. Limitations may arise, for instance, due to knowledge constraints with respect to the processes we are modelling, or computational constraints as to what can be feasibly modelled [1, 21, 22]. For example, some processes (e.g. political, cultural, and institutional) that are difficult to model oftentimes are not modelled because of these difficulties [20]. Alongside these, a model's applicability is very likely to be contextually limited. In this regard, there are many examples of problems arising when 'experts' have applied explanations out of context [23], or when attempts have been made to make 'predictions' by drawing on observations under 'similar' conditions elsewhere [24]. Though some of these limitations are unavoidable, recognising them may help navigate other modelling pitfalls. Continually reviewing the suitability and usefulness of models (and the sub-models they contain), alongside running the model under different considerations e.g. its sensitivity analysis, may help circumvent the latter (more avoidable) limitations.

Uncertainty

There are multiple layers of uncertainty to be considered when modelling aspects of the world.[1] Some of these (though not all) will be related to our knowledge. For instance, there may be limitations with respect to our data, or inadequacies regarding our understanding of the processes being modelled [1, 16]. Alongside this, there will also be 'model uncertainties' relating to the question as to whether the model bears any relation to the world 'out there' [25]. In this sense, knowledge is always partial, and evidence is often open to various interpretations [26]. These uncertainties usually increase with the complexity of the system we are trying to understand, and the number of perspectives that are brought to bear on it. Failing to acknowledge these

---

[1] Uncertainty is understood here as a situation where we don't know what we don't know [24, 52].

uncertainties, and partialities, or downplaying them—as is often the tendency in the public realm [20, 24]—is a further pitfall a modeller can fall into, and one that is likely to provide fuel for sceptics, reduce rather than expand the available options [27], and manifest later as 'surprises' [28].

Giving a False Sense of Security

Sometimes introducing a model into the policy process, especially one that promises prediction, simply opens up space for a lack of action [1]. In this sense, models can lure us into a false sense of security and actually prevent us from doing anything useful, safe in the illusion that we can predict and hence manage future changes [24]. If we have a tool that can provide us with some forecasts, there is the risk of relying on this, and thus avoid responsibility for perhaps the worst-case scenario or the unknown scenario. In this respect, at both the modelling and policy levels, there is a tendency to focus on the best-case/most tolerable scenario and use a model to justify this restricted focus, rather than consider the full range of possibilities. Models in this regard can sometimes act as 'symbolic substitutes' for action, and work to gloss over ideological premises [29], providing instead reassurance for a particular worldview, alongside justification for a particular course of action [25].

Narrowing the Evidential Base

As we saw with the case of the Newfoundland cod, although formal models can help us think about and understand things in a way we might not otherwise be able to do, they can also work to constrain the evidence base also, by side-lining other (perhaps less formal) forms of evidence. Sometimes other sources of evidence may be better suited to a task, than that which can be captured by a formal model—even one that is not constrained by the demands of analytical mathematics. In this sense, formalisation can lead to the exclusion of important nuances of a problem, oftentimes relating to processes that can be difficult to model, or value-based based issues on which there is no consensus. This might seem obvious, however, it becomes problematic in the sense that there is a tendency (discussed below) in policy-making to prioritise technical data (numerical data and the output of formal models) over other sources of evidence [30, p. 163]. It has been suggested elsewhere, that complex models may actually work to exacerbate this [31], which could work to further marginalise others forms of knowledge e.g. qualitative or local, place-based knowledge.

Inappropriate Focus on 'Facts' Rather than Values

Over the past number of decades value based questions have increasingly been redefined as technical issues that can be solved through science [1, 26]. What this glosses over, however, is that knowledge (including scientific knowledge) is rarely completely independent of values [23]. Almost all models (even formal models) contain subjective judgements, and elements of normative social theorising [17] – especially when dealing with complex social or ecological situations. Whilst the use of expertise to inform policy in itself reflects certain values with respect to what constitutes evidence [23]. In this sense, the boundary between science and policy is fuzzier than is often acknowledged [1, 23]. Already existing research agendas complicate this further [12], as do the existence of multiple frames of analysis and thus interpretations of the problem, some of which will be incommensurable [29]. Though models can provide advice in this process, they cannot offer resolution to the value based disputes that define the political realm (which is a large part of the policy-making process) [26]. What often happens, however, is that a technical model—by focusing our attention on the 'knowable' [32]—can work to conceal these value-laden issues, and depoliticise this process [1, 33, 34].

Failing to Understand the Policy-Making Process

There is a tendency (as discussed further below) to view the policy-making process as a linear process whereby a problem is (a) identified, (b) research is conducted, concrete evidence is supplied, which is (c) then used by policymakers to decide on the best way forward amidst competing interests. However, there is a lot of evidence to suggest that this is an oversimplified depiction of this process [1, 20, 26, 35]. Whilst experts do have a privileged role in forming policy, policies rarely flow directly from 'facts' [23]. In contrast, what often happens is that 'facts' can be used to legitimate particular courses of action [1, 26]. This is because the policy-making process is neither driven by 'rational analysis' or 'expert judgement' (nor should it be), but by 'public' debate over competing interests and values (i.e. this is democratic politics) [1, 26]. The goals of the policy might not be agreed on by all, and the extent to which the model complements or contradicts these goals will in large part determine whether it is accepted or rejected by policymakers [26]. For instance, some have suggested that the reason neoclassical economics has been so successful is that it provides an ideological function, rather than being empirically accurate [25].

A Summary of Pitfalls

Pitfall	Mitigating steps
Institutionalised assumptions	Be explicit about assumptions
Theoretical spectacles	All assumptions should be subject to independent and reflexive examination
Model spread	Critically assess already existing models, even those that are taken-for-granted
Confusions over model purpose	Decide what the purpose of your model is
Not knowing model limitations	Continually review the model, including the sub-models it contains
Uncertainty	Accept the uncertainty and be honest about it, in a manner that is not ambiguous
Giving a false sense of security	Don't oversell your model
Narrowing the evidential base	Not all knowledge seek formalisation!
Inappropriate focus on 'facts' rather than values	Is this simply an empirical question? Or is it also a normative one? (It's probably both)
Failing to understand the policy-making process	How is my model likely to be used in this process?

3 The Engineering/Predictive Paradigm for Policy Making

A common normative view of policy making (e.g. as described in the UK government's "Magenta Book" [36]) goes as follows:

1. Key performance indicators (KPIs) are designed to measure progress in obtaining policy goals (which are taken as given)
2. The possible policy options are described precisely
3. These are evaluated in terms of their *predicted* costs and benefits
4. The best policy is chosen and tried

This policy-choice process might then be embedded within an iterative approach which repeatedly (or occasionally) involves (a) evaluating current policies, (b) comparing the current policy against alternatives (using 2–4 above) and (c) changing or adapting the policy if this promises an improvement in outcomes.

Often, agent-based models are conceived of as helping policymakers in step 3 above, namely *predicting* the outcomes of different policies so that they can be systematically compared (usually using KPIs which can be estimated from model outcomes). Sometimes this is called "policy modelling", "model-based policy evaluation" or simply a "what if" analysis. I call this the "engineering paradigm" because it is analogous to the processes that are involved in engineering physical structures such as buildings or bridges.

MABS comes into the picture when it is perceived that simpler kinds of model are inadequate to doing the prediction that is needed in step 3 above. In other words, it is realised that the phenomena of concern is *complex*. Since MABS have the ability to represent sets of interacting agents, and explore the outcomes of different structures and behavioural rules, the hope is that such simulations will be able to provide the prediction that simpler models cannot. Thus, though the technology (and maybe the applicability) of MABS differs from previous modelling techniques, its role is the same.

However, it is unlikely that most MABS are able to fulfil this role. There are several reasons for this, including the following.

- Too many of the assumptions that go into the MABS are unreliable, for example aspects of agent decision-making in the simulation. Clearly, the more these aspects are based on good evidence, then this problem is reduced, however almost all MABS have so many assumptions that many unreliable (or even unquestioned) assumptions will remain.
- A fundamental kind of assumption is the list of those mechanisms that make it into the model and those that do not. There is no general meta-theory that tells us when we need any of a range of mechanisms (semantic communication, social norms, social influence, reputation, power, habit, practices etc. etc.). So it might be that if we miss one of these out that we totally alter the model results. A particular case of this is when we have not even thought of a mechanism or factor that turns out to be crucial later.
- The uncertainty in the target phenomena might be too great for prediction to be feasible. This may be due to a lack of adequate data or knowledge about key elements of the system, or it may be due to emergent chaotic outcomes that are produced by the system itself (however much one knows about it).

In practice, true prediction (that is, reliably anticipating data that is *unknown* to the modeller to a useful degree of accuracy) has turned out to be infeasible for most social phenomena[2]. However, despite this deficiency (in terms of the predictive ability necessary to making this paradigm *actually* work) does not stop researchers and analysts implying that they can do this. There seems a reluctance to tell policy actors (or grant-giving bodies) the truth – that such prediction will not be achieved[3].

The point is that, if you cannot predict (and hence evaluate) the impact of policy, this paradigm does not work. This raises the question as to what the alternatives might be? In particular, whether there is any positive role for MABS in policy. In the next section, we propose one.

4   Using Agent-Based Modelling for Uncertainty Analysis

Rather than predict what will happen, or even the probability distribution for what will happen, we suggest that a MABS is used to anticipate the various things that could happen. That is, move from a *probabilistic* approach to a *possibilistic* one. Assuming a MABS captures some of the complexity of what is being modelled, then some of the sequences of outcomes might be indicated in different runs of the simulation model. Note that such a simulation will not capture *all* of the possible outcomes – just some of them – thus it might not anticipate what *does* transpire. However, it could potentially map out more of the possibilities than those that could be envisaged without the modelling.

The usefulness of such an exercise is that it can inform a better *uncertainty analysis* of a situation or a policy. A risk-analysis estimates the probability of a known event occurring (usually something going wrong), an uncertainty analysis reveals some of the outcomes that one would not otherwise have planned for[4]. An analysis of the model runs should enable for the identification of a number of different kinds of outcome, each due to a different combination of processes.

Thus, whilst statistical and other methods might make predictions as to policy outcomes, a MABS might provide an accompanying analysis of the ways in which the policy might go unexpectedly wrong. Such an analysis can inform policy making and allow contingency planning if these outcomes are undesirable.

Once these possible outcomes have been identified, then the simulation can also be used to design ways of measuring the emergence of these outcomes. Equivalent measurement instruments can be implemented in the real situation to give the earliest possible warning of the emergence of deleterious outcomes. Such 'early warning' indicators and advance planning for these outcomes can allow policymakers to react in a more-timely manner, and hence mitigate the impact of these outcomes. In other words, such instruments can allow policymakers to better 'steer' or adapt policy.

---

[2] This does not mean it is impossible as [53] shows, or that we should not try to predict [54], but that it is only feasible in cases with limited set of outcomes and lots of data. There are no cases I know of where MABS have been predictively reliable.

[3] Sometimes it is merely implied that prediction is possible using evasive or unclear language, e.g. meaning prediction of model results only, but allowing the stakeholder to think this means prediction of aspects of reality.

[4] The risk vs. uncertainty distinction was originally made by Knight [55].

Knowledge of a wider set of possibilities than those of just the status quo and the desired outcome can help inform the wider political debate. Thus instead of the success of a policy being the sole domain of a policymaker, a more informed discussion of the risks as well as the claimed benefits might be conducted by a more extensive set of stakeholders. Unlike with simpler models used for prediction, such an approach might widen, rather than narrow, the consideration of issues surrounding a proposed policy.

An Example – Fisheries

Fisheries management is an area where that pressure to predict has been particularly acute, and it has been argued that in the quest to do so ecological realism was sacrificed [2, 3, 37, 38]. Most fisheries management policies today are based upon, in one way or another, single stock assessments, calculations of maximum sustainable yield (MSY), and the allocation of quotas [4, 39–42]. What this necessitates practically is calculating the number of fish that are in the sea [4], and predicting the number of fish that will be produced each year by those that are left uncaught [43, p. 79]. Much of this assessment work is dominated by mathematical modelling of a particular kind.

This approach to nature has by now been widely critiqued with respect to its underpinning assumptions, and its practical failures. Built upon a number of partial theories (some of which are bio-economic hybrids combining both natural and economic 'laws' [44]), it assumes that nature can be understood by mechanistic laws, behaves deterministically, tends towards stability (and that humans have a role in maintaining this equilibrium), may be isolated and understood as single components, predicted and controlled, amongst others [2, 4, 5, 39, 43–46].[5]

Though we know today there are many problems with viewing nature in this manner [43], and sustained yield approaches to the management of natural resources (including fisheries) have garnered much critique [2, 4, 44–46] (precipitating shifts towards the development and application of alternative approaches to resource management), this approach to fisheries has become so institutionalized (both within fisheries science, and international policy), that by and large it continues to provide the basis for much policy in this area [2, 4, 5, 46]. As seen with the case of the Newfoundland cod stocks [3, 5], and others [4, 46], however, such an approach has oftentimes proven disastrous.

Thus, to illustrate the use of simulation for an uncertainty analysis, we applied an existing socio-ecological test bed [47] to look at the possible effects different fishing regimes may have on the underlying ecology. This is *not* to predict the effects of these regimes (even the average or expected outcomes), but look at the possible ways such regimes could go wrong.

Instead of modelling a few specific species, this test-bed allows for the evolution of a multi-species ecology which is constantly evolving and where the species are constantly interacting. We do not have space to explain this model in this short chapter, but refer readers to [47] for a more detailed explication.

---

[5] Some of these assumptions, it has been argued, are more tightly related to the demands of mathematics, and the capacities of quantitative models, than anything else [38]. Alongside this, historians have been astute in highlighting that part of the reason this approach to fisheries gained such traction was that it provided an approach that was in line with a number of political and economic objectives [4].

In the version used here, plants and higher order trophic levels (fish) are distinguished – the plants compete for limited resources from the patches, and other individuals either eat the plants or each other for energy. The affordances between individuals and each other (or the patches they inhabit) follows [48] and has been shown (in other models) to result in the evolution of food webs with many of the characteristics of observed food webs [49]. The model consists of a 2D grid of well-mixed patches in which individuals can interact. This is illustrated in Fig. 1.

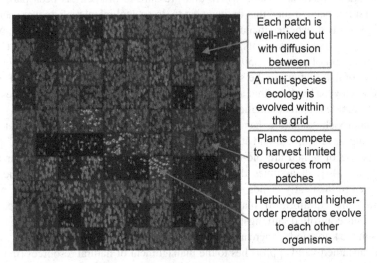

Fig. 1. A multispecies, evolving fisheries model using a 2D grid of well-mixed patches

To produce a complex ecology of plant and fish species we evolve the whole ecosystem from scratch using an analogue of genetic evolution – starting with plants, then introducing herbivores and allowing higher predators to evolve from these. This complex ecology is then 'saved' for use as a consistent starting point for explorations of the impact of different catchment policies (or none). This is illustrated in Fig. 2.

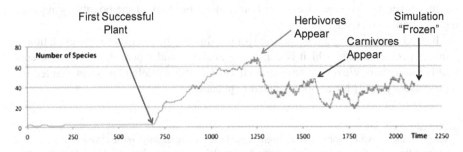

Fig. 2. Evolving a complex ecosystem of species which is 'saved' as a consistent starting point for multiple runs under different extraction regimes (or none)

We then run the simulation starting in this exact state many times using different random seeds and applying different exogenous fishing extraction patterns to it. By examining the 'trajectory' of the runs over many 'future' simulation time intervals (ticks) we can see some of the possible outcomes of that policy and compare these against those of the null cases (no fishing).

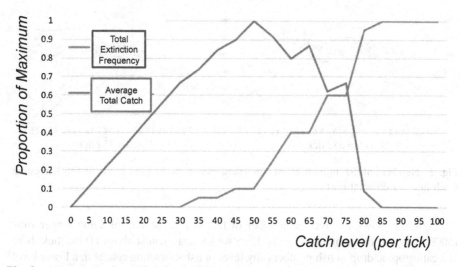

Fig. 3. Average over last 100 ticks and 20 simulation runs for different levels of extraction of: (blue line) whether all species were extinct (orange line) total fish caught (Color figure online)

To illustrate the model and its use, we run the model 20 times over 1000 more ticks at different levels of fish extraction, and look at the outcomes either over that time, or at the end of the runs.

Figure 3 shows a summary of the outcomes over the last 100 of those ticks (i.e. at the end of the run) summed over those runs and scaled by the maximum value that occurs. There the orange line shows a classic extraction curve with the greatest average catchment being at a level of 50 fish per tick caught. However the blue line shows the proportion of runs in which all fish had gone extinct by this time, and one can see that there was total extinction in at least one run at all levels of fish extraction above 30 fish/tick. In this model, at least, maximising "sustainable" fishing levels risks total extinction.

For the reasons why this apparent contradiction can occur, we need to look at some of the detail of the runs. One of the advantages of this approach is that we do not have to rely on average or equilibrium levels but can see some of the extremes that can occur dependent on the vagaries of chance and interspecies interaction.

Figure 4 shows the number of fish in each simulation over time, for two different levels of catchment (25 fish per tick and 35 fish per tick). Here one can see that although the fishing is done at a uniform rate, the number of fish varies chaotically all the time. This is true for this model even in cases where there is no fish extraction at all. What seems to be happening is that (a) fish numbers vary all the time up and down and

(b) fish extraction creates a 'danger zone' at low fish levels – the higher the extraction rate the wider the zone. When fish levels wander into this zone rapid extinction of all fish occurs (as you can see at the right hand side of Fig. 4 at 35 fish/tick extraction). Remember these are total fish statistics over all species present – if we looked into the variation of each species in each run, even more variation would be revealed.

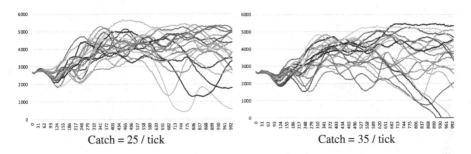

Fig. 4. Numbers of fish in each of 20 simulation runs with different levels of fish harvesting (each line is a different run)

Figure 5 shows the average number of fish left at the end of some longer runs (5000 ticks) for different catch levels. Here we see that, whilst above 60 fish/tick there is a catastrophic drop in fish numbers any level of fish extraction results in a lower level of fish (this is confirmed by more detailed series of runs done at low levels of fish extraction). That is, fish levels do not totally 'recover' when they are being constantly extracted. Similar results hold when the number of fish species are measured. In this model, at least, there is no threshold for fishing below which is safe – in any mature complex ecology there are always some species that are marginal and will be wiped out by even low levels of fishing. There is also, interestingly, no observable equilibria – if you continue running this model the lines do not 'settle down' but continue to gyrate.

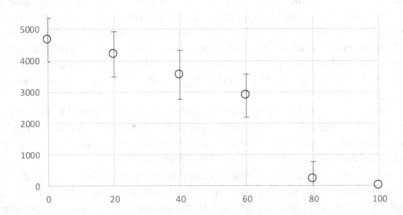

Fig. 5. Average number of fish at end of 5000 simulation ticks for different levels of catch with standard error bars (over 20 independent runs for each catch level)

Finally, we compare two methods of fish extraction: (a) a random uniform method of extraction (as used in all the above examples) and (b) a patch-by-patch method (where fishing is done by selecting a patch at random, taking all the fish there – or how much of the catch is left if less – then selecting another etc. until the quota is reached).

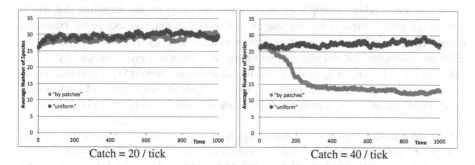

Fig. 6. Average number of species over time and 20 runs, comparing a uniform, random method (red line) of catch compared to a patch-by-patch approach (blue line) (Color figure online)

Figure 6 shows the average number of species over time for 20 runs over 1000 ticks for each of these options. In this version of the model, at lower levels of extraction each method has a similar impact on the number of species (on average), but at higher levels (40 fish/tick), there is a significant difference. Thus it could be that it is not just the *amount* of fish extracted that matters, but the *pattern* of that extraction.

We do not know if the complex ecologies being tested against are like the observed ones, these models do not predict the result of policy. But they do show plausible complex dynamics that cannot be ruled out in real, dynamic multispecies ecologies. They also illustrate what *might* happen when we move outside the realm of over-simple models and assumptions. Such an exercise could help warn us of some of the things that could go wrong in fisheries, for example that changing the patterns of how fish are caught might cause fish extinctions, even if the number of fish being remains constant.

5   Concluding Discussion

It is in the nature of many complex systems that we will never exhaustively know them [32, 50]. As we have seen, taking the road that pretends otherwise is fraught with dangers. Though it is unlikely that the partialities of our knowledge will be overcome, we have suggested a way that MABs might be used in a manner that could widen, rather than narrow, the consideration of issues surrounding a potential policy. To this end, we have proposed a process of *reflexive possibilistic modelling*. Rather than working to take the politics out of policy [1], such an approach, we hope, might provide a tool to assess future options under a range of scenarios, and from a range of perspectives.

That said, formal modelling approaches alone, even those that are reflexive and possibilistic, are unlikely to widen the possibilities within a policy-making process of limited reflexivity, where a multiplicity of perspectives are either not recognised or are systematically suppressed. Conversely, a process that encouraged open and transparent public debate with respect to the benefits, costs and uncertainties of different policy options (which would entail exposing the contingencies of our knowledge and the assumptions embedded within our methodologies) might, regardless of the quality of the modelling [17, 24, 35].

In this sense, taking multiplicity and plurality seriously means accepting that whilst models are useful, there is no one source of knowledge that can dictate the course of action under conditions of socio-environmental complexity [1]. In these instances different interpretations and interests will exist, and often the value frames of different actors in the policy-making process will be 'incommensurable' [51]. From this angle, forcing a consensual vision or model [1] would negate the importance of contestation for debating these values within the framework of democratic politics [51].

Acknowledgements. The authors acknowledge funding from the EU's Marie-Curie Horizon 2020 program as part of the Social Science Aspects of Fisheries for the 21st Century (SAF21) project, number 642080. We thank all those with whom we have had useful discussions on these subjects, including those at the University of Tromsø and at the MABS international workshop in Stockholm, July 2018.

References

1. Sarewitz, D.: Science and environmental policy: an excess of objectivity. In: Earth Matters: The Earth Sciences, Philosophy, and the Claims of Community, pp. 79–98 (2000)
2. Bavington, D.: Managed Annihilation: An Unnatural History of the Newfoundland Cod Collapse. UBC Press, Vancouver (2010)
3. Finlayson, A.C.: Fishing for Truth : A Sociological Analysis of Northern Cod Stock Assessments from 1977 to 1990. Institute of Social and Economic Research, Memorial University of Newfoundland (1994)
4. Finley, C.: All the Fish in the Sea: Maximum Sustainable Yield and the Failure of Fisheries Management. The University of Chicago Press, Chicago (2011)
5. Bavington, D.: Marine and freshwater fisheries in Canada: uncertainties, conflicts, and hope on the water. In: Resource and Environmental Management in Canada, pp. 221–245. Oxford University Press, Don Mills (2015)
6. Harris, L.: Independent Review of the State of the Northern Cod Stock Executive Summary and Recommendations (1990)
7. Aodha, L., Edmonds, B.: Some pitfalls to beware when applying models to issues of policy relevance. In: Edmonds, B., Meyer, R. (eds.) Simulating Social Complexity. UCS, pp. 801–822. Springer, Cham (2017). https://doi.org/10.1007/978-3-319-66948-9_29
8. Conte, R., Edmonds, B., Moss, S., Sawyer, R.K.: Sociology and social theory in agent based social simulation: a symposium. Comput. Math. Organ. Theory **7**(3), 183–205 (2001)
9. Saltelli, A., Funtowicz, S.: When all models are wrong. Issues Sci. Technol. **30**, 79–85 (2014)
10. Sterman, J.D.: All models are wrong: reflections on becoming a systems scientist. Syst. Dyn. Rev. **18**(4), 501–531 (2002)
11. Forsyth, T.: Critical Political Ecology: The Politics of Environmental Science. Routledge, Abingdon (2003)
12. Jasanoff, S.: (No?) Accounting for expertise. Sci. Public Policy **30**(3), 157–162 (2003)

13. Epstein, B.: Agent-based modeling and the fallacies of individualism. In: Models Simulations and Representations, pp. 115–144. Routledge (2013)
14. Glynn, P.D.: Integrated environmental modelling: human decisions, human challenges. Geol. Soc. London Spec. Publ. **408**(1), 161–182 (2017)
15. Kuhn, T.S.: The Structure of Scientific Revolutions. The University of Chicago Press, Chicago (1962)
16. Lahsen, M.: Seductive simulations? Uncertainty distribution around climate models. Soc. Stud. Sci. **35**(6), 895–922 (2005)
17. Evans, R.: Economic models and policy advice: theory choice or moral choice? Sci. Context **12**(02), 351–376 (1999)
18. Wynne, B.: Risk and environment as legitimatory discourses of technology: reflexivity inside out? Curr. Sociol. **50**(3), 459–477 (2002)
19. Edmonds, B.: Different modelling purposes. In: Edmonds, B., Meyer, R. (eds.) Simulating Social Complexity. UCS, pp. 39–58. Springer, Cham (2017). https://doi.org/10.1007/978-3-319-66948-9_4
20. Shackley, S., Wynne, B.: Representing uncertainty in global climate change science and policy: devices and authority. Sci. Technol. Hum. Values **21**(3), 275–302 (1996)
21. Sismondo, S.: Models, simulations, and their objects. Sci. Context **12**(2), 247–260 (2017)
22. Winsberg, E.: Sanctioning models: the epistemology of simulation. Sci. Context **12**(2), 275–292 (1999)
23. Forsyth, T.: Expertise needs transparency not blind trust: a deliberative approach to integrating science and social participation. Crit. Policy Stud. **5**(3), 317–322 (2011)
24. Wynne, B.: Uncertainty and environmental learning. Reconceiving science and policy in the preventive paradigm. Glob. Environ. Chang. **2**(2), 111–127 (1992)
25. Ravetz, J.R.: Economics as an elite folk science: the suppression of uncertainty. J. Post Keynes. Econ. **17**(2), 165–184 (1994)
26. Heazle, M.: Uncertainty in Policy Making: Values and Evidence in Complex Decisions. Routledge, Abingdon (2012)
27. Saltelli, A., Stark, P.B., Becker, W., Stano, P.: Climate models as economic guides scientific challenge or quixotic quest? Issues Sci. Technol. **31**(3), 79–84 (2015)
28. Pellizzoni, L.: Knowledge, uncertainty and the transformation of the public sphere. Eur. J. Soc. Theory **6**(3), 327–355 (2003)
29. Dryzek, J.S.: Policy analysis and planning: from science to argument. In: The Argumentative Turn in Policy Analysis and Planning, pp. 213–231. Routledge (1993)
30. Pearce, W., Wesselink, A., Colebatch, H.: Evidence and meaning in policy making. Evid. Policy A J. Res. Debate Pract. **10**(2), 161–165 (2014)
31. Saltelli, A., Giampietro, M.: What is wrong with evidence based policy, and how can it be improved? Futures **91**, 62–71 (2017)
32. Jasanoff, S.: Technologies of humility: researchers and policy-makers need ways for accommodating the partiality of scientific knowledge and for acting under the inevitable uncertainty it holds. Nature **450**(7166), 33–34 (2007)
33. Benessia, A., et al.: The Rightful Place of Science: Science on the Verge. Consortium for Science. Policy & Outcomes, Tempe (2016)
34. Forsyth, T.: Politicizing environmental science does not mean denying climate science nor endorsing it without question. Glob. Environ. Polit. **12**(2), 18–23 (2012)
35. Shackley, S., Wynne, B.: Integrating knowledges for climate change: pyramids, nets and uncertainties. Glob. Environ. Chang. **5**(2), 113–126 (1995)
36. Treasury, H.M.: The Magenta Book: Guidance for Evaluation. UK Government (2011). https://www.gov.uk/government/publications/the-magenta-book

37. Holm, P.: Crossing the border: on the relationship between science and fishermen's knowledge in a resource management context. Marit. Stud. **2**(1), 5–33 (2003)
38. Francis, R.C.: Fisheries science now and in the future: a personal view. New Zeal. J. Mar. Freshw. Res. **14**(1), 95–100 (1980)
39. Nielsen, K.N., Holm, P.: A brief catalogue of failures: framing evaluation and learning in fisheries resource management. Mar. Policy **31**(6), 669–680 (2007)
40. Smith, T.: Scaling Fisheries: The Science of Measuring the Effects of Fishing, 1855–1955. Cambridge University Press, Cambridge (1994)
41. Campling, L., Havice, E., McCall Howard, P.: The political economy and ecology of capture fisheries: market dynamics, resource access and relations of exploitation and resistance. J. Agrar. Chang. **12**(2–3), 177–203 (2012)
42. Winder, G.M.: Introduction: fisheries, quota management, quota transfer and bio-economic rationalization. In: Winder, Gordon M. (ed.) Fisheries, Quota Management and Quota Transfer. MPS, vol. 15, pp. 3–28. Springer, Cham (2018). https://doi.org/10.1007/978-3-319-59169-8_1
43. Bocking, S.: Nature's Experts: Science, Politics, and the Environment. Rutgers University Press, New Brunswick (2004)
44. Hubbard, J.: Fisheries biology and the dismal science: economists and the rational exploitation of fisheries for social progress. In: Winder, G. (ed.) Fisheries, Quota Management and Quota Transfer. MPS, vol. 15, pp. 31–61. Springer, Cham (2018). https://doi.org/10.1007/978-3-319-59169-8_2
45. Hubbard, J.: Mediating the North Atlantic environment: fisheries biologists, technology, and marine spaces. Environ. Hist. **18**(1), 88–100 (2013)
46. Pilkey, O.H., Pilkey-Jarvis, L.: Useless Arithmetic: Why Environmental Scientists Can't Predict the Future. Columbia University Press, New York (2007)
47. Edmonds, B.: A socio-ecological test bed. Ecol. Complex. (2018, in press)
48. Caldarelli, G., Higgs, P.G., McKane, A.J.: Modelling coevolution in multispecies communities. J. Theor. Biol. **193**, 345–358 (1998)
49. McKane, A.J.: Evolving complex food webs. Eur. Phys. J. B **38**, 287–295 (2004)
50. Pickering, A.: The Cybernetic Brain: Sketches of Another Future. University of Chicago Press, Chicago (2010)
51. Matulis, B.S., Moyer, J.R.: Beyond inclusive conservation: the value of pluralism, the need for agonism, and the case for social instrumentalism. Conserv. Lett. **10**(3), 279–287 (2017)
52. Mehta, L., Leach, M., Newell, P., Scoones, I., Sivaramakrishnan, K., Way, S.-A.: Exploring understandings of institutions and uncertainty: new directions in natural resource management, IDS Discussion Paper 372, vol. 1, pp. 1–48 (1999)
53. Silver, N.: The Signal and the Noise: Why so Many Predictions Fail–but Some Don't. Penguin Press, London (2012)
54. Polhill, G.: Why the social simulation community should tackle prediction. Rev. Artif. Soc. Soc. Simul. (2018). https://rofasss.org/2018/08/06/gp/
55. Knight, F.: Risk, Uncertainty and Profit. Hart Schaffner and Marx, New York (1921)

A Comparison of Two Historical Trader Societies – An Agent-Based Simulation Study of English East India Company and New-Julfa

Amir Hosein Afshar Sedigh[1]([⊠]), Christopher K. Frantz[2],
Bastin Tony Roy Savarimuthu[1], Martin K. Purvis[1], and Maryam A. Purvis[1]

[1] Department of Information Science, University of Otago, Dunedin, New Zealand
amir.afshar@postgrad.otago.ac.nz,
{tony.savarimuthu,martin.purvis,maryam.purvis}@otago.ac.nz
[2] Department of Computer Science, Norwegian University of Science and
Technology, Gjøvik, Norway
christopher.frantz@ntnu.no

Abstract. In this paper, we study the English East India Company (EIC) and Armenian traders of New-Julfa (Julfa) that were active during 17th and 18th centuries. Both were successful trading cooperatives that relied on different institutional parameters and mechanisms to coordinate their activities. In this work, we explore a selection of those aspects (five of them): (a) societal mortality rate, (b) nature of the system in attracting workforce (open vs. close), (c) existence of adjudication process, (d) payment scheme, and (e) punishment. To study effects of these attributes on system behaviour, we systematically modify these attributes to create a total of 10 hypothetical systems, two of which mirror characteristics of the EIC and Julfa systems. By doing these modifications, we study which of these systems are successful in improving system performance in terms of (a) identifying cheaters, (b) improving trading skills of agents, (c) making more profit for the organisation, and (d) deterring agents from cheating. A central insight of the simulation was the impact of substantial profit sharing on trader cooperation (i.e. more profit sharing resulted in lowered cheating). Moreover, our results show that Julfa had a lower number of cheaters despite having an open workforce to attract employees, thus making it more profitable and robust to changes in workforce characteristics (i.e. using an open workforce society).

Keywords: Principal-agent problem ·
Armenian traders of New-Julfa · Agent based modelling ·
English East India Company · Game theory · Social simulations ·
Historical trading

1 Introduction

One of the issues faced by international companies in a collaborative and distributed environment is limited information transparency, often leading to

© Springer Nature Switzerland AG 2019
P. Davidsson and H. Verhagen (Eds.): MABS 2018, LNAI 11463, pp. 17–31, 2019.
https://doi.org/10.1007/978-3-030-22270-3_2

information asymmetry. Nowadays, international companies try to overcome this problem using real-time information infrastructures. Challenges associated with such a class of problem are commonly referred to as the *"principal-agent problem"* [14], wherein two parties are engaged in a deal where an *agent* should pursue his *principal*'s (Master's) benefits by performing actions, but these actions are hard to monitor. Particularly in long distance trades that we consider in this work, the power delegation to agents (i.e. access to company resources) and absence of transparency are some reasons for using company resources for self-interests. Henceforth, we refer to any selfish behaviour that imposes some costs to the principal as **cheating**.

Note that, agents are important organisation resources because their gradual improvement of skills leads to a company profitability enhancement. On the other hand, retain skilled agents cheating impose coasts to the organisation. We study these effects, by modelling some aspects of *English East India company* (EIC) and *Armenian merchants of New-Julfa* (Julfa). These societies were long-distance traders that pursued their benefits by delegating some rights to agents in remote places. They were successful in trade, despite their different demographic and institutional characteristics, namely workforce society, punishment and reward, and mortality rate (we use institutions as a term reflecting rules and norms in organisations [17]). The reason for choosing these societies with these characteristics lies in extensive studies performed by historians about them that provides insights into their institutions, their differences in managing their own societies, and their awareness about each other's policies. What makes the comparison of both systems appealing is their evident co-existence on the Indian subcontinent, with EIC managers identifying the Julfa traders as superior. So, EIC granted Julfans same privileges as British merchants to "alter and invert the ancient course of their trade to and from Europe" [2]. This study aims to unlock some of the secrets of this *ancient course*.

We employ agent-based simulation to study the two societies. While prior work has investigated other trading societies (e.g. Maghribi and Genoese) [6], our work here is quite different in characteristics and also considers different societies. The rest of this paper is organised as follows: Sect. 2 takes a comparative look at EIC and Julfa. Section 3 discusses how these systems are abstractly modelled and the reason behind chosen parameters. In Sect. 4 results of simulation are presented and discussed. Finally, Sect. 5 sums up the findings of the model and proposes future directions.

2   Review of Systems

In this section we provide a brief background of the two systems and then compare them with respect to five characteristics of EIC and Julfa. A brief review of these characteristics is presented in Table 1. EIC was formed in 1600 based on monopoly of trade between Asia and Britain, granted by Queen Elizabeth I [20] and was active until middle of the 19th century. One of the first problems EIC faced was finding experienced agents to perform long-distance trades. So, they used an *open* workforce scheme for subsequent years where any worker from Britain was allowed to join. On the other hand, Armenian merchants of New-Julfa were originally from Old-Julfa in Armenia, and they had inheritance rules that created strong family bonds [12], and used informal institutions to control society. These kinds of social bonds and sharing the same background were some reasons of having a *closed* workforce society in Julfa. Note that, both societies hired males as agents (we focus on men in societies).

Moreover, some relaxations of EIC monopoly between 1660 and 1700 that followed by the establishment of *Company of Scotland* in 1695 [5], persuaded the company to pay low nominal salaries[1] and grant agents privilege of private trade (right of trade in the intra-Asian market) [10]. As a result, EIC agents sought other sources to increase their income and counted on private trade as their real salary [10]. In Julfa masters used commenda contract (an open-ended contract with substantial profit sharing) where a proportion of profit (around 30%) was shared with traders [12]. The mortality rate of EIC was higher. A newcomer to the system on average worked not even past his 30s (i.e. 15 years of service time) [10]. On the other hand, there are no discussions about such a problem for Julfan people, neither in their letters nor in historical contexts.

Table 1. System specification based on EIC and Julfa Societies

Characteristics	EIC	Julfa
Nature of the workforce	Open	Closed
Payment design	Private trade + living costs	Commenda + living costs
Mortality rate	High (H)	Low (L)
Adjudication chance	No	Yes
Punishment	Dismissal + unutilised bond	Boycotting, losing family or pay costs + interest

Julfans had autonomy inside and outside of Iran and established churches of their own in their frequently visited cities and used them as a source for storing (archiving) and transmitting information [2]. Moreover, they had two kinds of institutions for settling disputes, the assembly of merchants and portable courts. We call the process of going through evidences and decision making the *adjudication* process. This process was rigorous and identified cheaters effectively. However, in EIC managers felt that a large number of cheaters were present in the system despite limited reports [3]. This could have been from colluding together or increased tolerance in managers towards cheating to avoid hiring unqualified people [3]. However, this insufficient monitoring introduced a surprising firing pattern (i.e. more experienced merchants were fired in higher proposition despite their higher income[2]). So, in EIC subjective means for identifying

---

[1] £5 to £40 versus £50 in Britain.
[2] Around £1000 see Tables 1–3 of [11].

cheaters was employed without any adjudication process [11]. This firing scheme introduces likelihood of punishment for a bad performance without any evidences for cheating.

On the other hand, EIC discouraged employees from cheating by asking them to provide a bond of at least £500 [11] and punished them by dismissing them in case of suspicion. However, in Julfa one of the frequently used ways of punishment was asking a cheater, or his core or extended family to pay back the incurred costs, otherwise they would be boycotted from future trades engagement. The evidence suggests that these consequences were harsh with a merchant noting to his brother: "I would rather chuse [sic] to dye [sic], than for them to [blot my] name out of the list [2]."

In the closed society of Julfa, there were several means of monitoring such as discussing merchants' behaviour expressed through letters written between different people, trustworthiness of other agents, and prices. For instance, we can see in one of the merchant's correspondence with his cousin (Paron Petros) which reads:

> Paron Petros, your letter from Livorno dated Atam 22 [May 11] reached us on Hamira 8 [November 23], and we became acquainted with your situation. [However] your letter was without flavor or salt [Bi Namak] (literally means "without salt") because it contained no news about purchases and expenditures. The salt in a merchant's letter is [the news about] purchases and expenditures. When you send us your next letter, be sure to write about the state of purchases and expenditures both in Livorno and Venice, so we too can be more satisfied.

"The Jullfans" also could gather information about activities of merchants using church archives or through direct contacts during meetings in local churches or chapels [2]. Finally, an agent upon his return has to hand over everything he has with him including goods, accounts, personal luggage, and clothing makes it harder to hide cheats from master [12]. These detailed communication plus their strong social relationships, convince us to assume non-cheaters followed Socrates arguments:

> ... Which is better, to live among bad citizens, or among good ones? ... Do not the good do their neighbours good, and the bad do them evil? ... And is there anyone who would rather be injured than benefited by those who live with him? [18]

As discussed above, these two societies had differences in workforce societies, payments, mortality rates, adjudication process and monitoring, and punishment (see Table 1) and we study effects of these differences in these systems using an agent-based simulation.

3   Simulation Model of Two Systems

In this section we present a model that investigates the effects of five key attributes of aforementioned societies on *system performance*. To do so, we assume that a part of society consists of people who play a game with incomplete information wherein they decide whether to cheat or not [16]. Agents make this decision based on parameters, such as cheating income (CI), future income (FI), discount rate (α), and punishment (P). Moreover, effectiveness of institutions has an effect on their decision making. In other words, probability associated with each situation (system state) affects agent behaviour. So, agents estimate the probability of getting fired in different situations: (a) cheating (pc), (b) bad performance associated with cheating (ppc), and (c) bad performance of non-cheaters (ppnc). Table 2 shows how agents decide about their *actual* actions based on the consequences and their estimations of their *master's suspicion* about what they did, i.e. they may not cheat but master may think they cheated based on their performance. Table 2a shows the utility obtained (punishment or reward) of each state. Table 2b shows the estimated probability of being in each state for chasing an action. The rest of the society are those who would not cheat at all for their moral, religious, or other reasons. Moreover, organisations aim at maximising profits employing different payment, punishment, and firing schemes.

Table 2. Game that potential cheaters play

(a)Punishment and Rewards			(b)Associated Probabilities		
	Master's Suspicion			Master's Suspicion	
	Cheat (C)	Not Cheated (NC)		C	NC
Actual C	$CI - P$	$CI + \alpha \times FI$	Actual C	$pc + ppc$	$1 - (pc + ppc)$
Actual NC	0	$\alpha \times FI$	Actual NC	$ppnc$	$1 - ppnc$

Algorithm 1. Organisational level

```
1  Identify and fire cheaters based on observations
   /* Observations is a function of agent's cheating level and chance of identification
   */
2  if There is no adjudication process then
3  │   Measure performance of agents based on their experience and update their record
   │   using discount factor
4  │   Fire worst performers with high access, i.e. Junior merchants, senior merchants, or
   │   council members (more than 12 years experience).
5  if Workfoce Society is open then
6  │   Hire People so that the population is stable
7  else
8  │   Hire all agents aged 15
9  Current Capital ← ∑∀Agents Master's capital in hand of agents
10 ROR ← Current Capital / Old Capital
11 Old Capital ← Current Capital
12 Redistribute capital
   /* It takes place based on the number of newcomers, fired, and deceased agents.
      First, managers allocate 100 to each new agent, then the remainder of accumulated
      capital would be distributed among other merchants considering their current
      access to company capital (i.e. their associated Master's capital, see Algorithm
      2)                                                                           */
```

We assume that these trader societies are managed by a manager entity (an abstraction for the whole organisation). The steps performed by master, is indicated in Algorithm 1. This algorithm shows how the organisational level of a system works. The firing of cheaters takes place as a function of effectiveness of monitoring mechanisms (line 1). Monitoring depends on information about agents' behaviour available to principal that is a function of employee's loyalty. We assume closedness of workforce society increases loyalty and information transparency due to the social bonds and informal and formal measures of information exchange. Another firing scheme is associated with lack of adjudication process (e.g. in case of EIC) and agents are judged based on their performance (lines 2–4). Then, organisations have different schemes of hiring. In open system, agents are hired to stabilise the population and in closed one all agents aged 15 years are hired (lines 5–8). The total capital in the society is the sum of capital available to all agents (line 9). Rate of Return (ROR) is the ratio of current to old capital (line 10). Then, the organisation updates its old capital for the next run (line 11) and redistributes capital based on the fired agents, deceased agents, newcomers, and agents current access to organisation's capital (line 12).

A simulation run starts with a predefined population with different ages and random priors for associated probabilities for each state. The age structure of initial population is defined in a way that it reflects the associated mortality rate. To do so, we fitted exponential function on data as suggested by [7]. Then, based on: (a) population of a given year, (b) percentage of deceased agents, and (c) assumption that the society population did not have any trend (i.e. increasing or decreasing) recently, the number of agents in subsequent years are identified. The results of this procedure is depicted in Fig. 1. For each run, which equals a year, agents update their assessments about effectiveness of different institutions, for instance the probabilities for a cheater or non-cheater to be fired. The main parameters they learn are shown in Table 3. Agents discount past estimation using 0.3 weight due to the one year lag and obsoleteness of past information.

Table 3. Punishment, reward, and learning

Parameter	Learning means	Note
Future income	Asking other agents	
Chance of being punished as a cheater	Observation	Discount past parameters
Chance of getting fired without any adjudication process	Observation	Discount past parameters
Chance of cheating	Observation	Discount past Performance
Effectiveness of bond	Observation	Bayesian
Punishment in commenda	Contract	Revealed Cheating + Interest

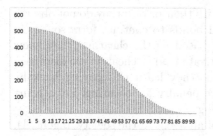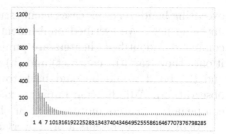

Fig. 1. Age structure for systems with (a) low mortality rate and (b) high mortality rate.

Algorithm 2. An agent's operational details

---

1 Increase Age by 1 year, die randomly considering mortality rate for age, to be fired based on the master's policy.
2 **if** *Workforce Society is* **open** *and mortality rate is* **high** **then**
3 ⎿ leave work with 40% chance × associated mortality rate according to age

4 **if** *age* >= 15 *and not fired* **then**
5   **if** *age* ∈ [16, 25] **then** increase skill (*s*) by 10% of maximum attainable skill
6   **if** *Workfoce Society is closed* **then**
7   **if** *(21 ≤ Age ≤ 55)* **then**
8   **if** *#kids is less than Maximum* **then**
9   **if** *rand() ≤ reproduction chance* **then**
10   ⎿ Create a new person with age = 0 and random parameters
11   ⎿ Increase number of kids by 1

12   Cheating cost = 0
13   **if** *potential cheater* **then**
      /* Calculate provisioned income, based on Master's and Agent's capital   */
14     $t \leftarrow 1$, cap(0) ← My capital, $I(0) \leftarrow 0$, For commenda Mcap(0) = Master's capital and Mcap(0) = 0 for the rest.
15   **while** $t \leq 6$ **do**
16       $I(t) \leftarrow (aai + aais \times s) \times [0.3 \times$ Mcap $(t-1) +$ cap $(t-1)]$
17   cap$(t) \leftarrow$ cap$(t-1) + I(t-1)$
18   Mcap$(t) \leftarrow (aai + aais \times s) \times 0.7 \times$ Mcap $(t-1)$
19   ⎿ $t \leftarrow t+1$
20   Discounted Income $(\alpha \times FI) \leftarrow \sum_{i=1}^{6} \alpha^i \times I(i)$
21   Consider a random manipulation (RM), $CI = RM$ for commenda and $CI = G(< RM)$ for others.
22   Learn pc, ppc, $ppnc$, and effectiveness of bond (eb).
23   **if**
      $(pc+ppc) \times (CI - eb \times pc \times P) + (1 - pc - ppnc) \times (CI + \alpha \times FI) > (1 - ppnc) \times \alpha \times FI$
      then
24   ⎿ Cheating cost = (RM)

25   **if** *Commenda* **then**
26   Master's capital ← $((Rand(aai) + Rand(irs) \times s) \times 0.7 \times$ Mcap $) -$ Cheating cost
27   **else**
28   ⎿ Master's capital ← $((Rand(aai) + Rand(irs) \times s) \times$ Mcap$) -$ Cheating cost

---

The only exception for this learning method relates to not-executed bonds. We know of no bond that were executed in EIC based on accumulated data, so agents increase their belief about ineffectiveness of these bonds with more evidence (they use a Bayesian inference for a Bernoulli distribution that assesses probability of executing bonds). For all cases agents stick with their prior if they do not observe anything new. We ascribed punishment and bonds to contract form so: (a) in commenda, identified cheaters are punished based on the cheating (they know it once they start the contract) and (b) in private trades, cheaters are dismissed and the bond would be paid back to them (they learn this paying back by observation). Adjudication impacts excessive penalty for cheating, i.e. a court can penalise cheaters more than their cheating.

Algorithm 2 represents a brief overview of an agent in the society, (agent A). A gets 1 year older, and based on the mortality rate associated with his age dies with a probability and stops working if he is fired. In a closed system a fired agent continues his presence in the system but cannot trade any more. This assumption was inspired by Julfa institutions, i.e. the closed workforce instance that we have. We employ it to prevent a closed society artificially becoming extinct (line 1). A high mortality rate in an open society causes a part of the society to prefer leaving the company for a healthier life back home (line 2–3). The rest of the algorithm is applicable for working agents (line 4 indicates this concept). A's skill (s) linearly improves during the first ten years until he reaches his maximum attainable skill (line 5). In a closed system, A reproduces another agent (male kid) while he is aged between 21 to 55 with a probability until he either has maximum possible kids or dies (line 6–11). Each new born agent has totally new parameters, i.e. he won't inherit bad reputation, skill, or cheating tendency.

We recalculate the cheating costs incurred to the system by agents per run (line 12). A potential cheater decides whether to cheat or not based on the afore-mentioned game (line 13–24). To do so, first A calculates his provisioned *reward* based on the form of the contract and considered time horizon and cumulated capital in subsequent iterations. So, A considers no Income for now ($I(0)$) and the effects of master's capital in commenda contract (line 14). Then, the reward is calculated based on the assessed average income (aai) plus average attainable income for skill ($aais$) multiplied by the degree of skill (s) for the considered time horizon (lines 15–19). A considers the near future in this calculation, in our simulation (6 years). Then, A discounts provisioned income using his discount factor (line 20). Cheating is considered by assuming that it is a random manip-ulation (RM) with a linear correlation to its visibility. This randomness reflects intuitions about more manipulation is more visible and available opportunities for manipulating orders. In the commenda the trader would make as much as the profit that he hides from his master, because he is the one who buys and sells the items. In EIC the agent's profit at most can be that much, since most of the time it was in the form of accepting a gift from other parties to change the orders[3] (line 21). Afterwards, A updates his estimations of probabilities of reactions to his current state based on observations and his prior and the effectiveness of bonds for EIC (line 22). Consequently, A decides either to cheat or not based on

---

[3] The most frequent reported cheats include embezzlement, making up Indian names to sell own items, accepting gift from brokers, i.e. choosing best gift giver or parties that work in private trades to increase bargain power for own benefits [15].

rewards, punishments, and other estimated parameters (line 23–24). Finally, A updates his capital as well as master's capital (line 25–28). Note that the master capital directly affects system profitability that is a function of payment scheme and cheating costs incurred by A and for commenda is 30% less due to the profit sharing.

Now we discuss parameters that were fixed in our simulation and reasons for choosing these numbers. The number of agents is defined based on the approximate society population. In Julfa around 800 traders (master and agents) were available at 17th century [2] and in EIC based on the number of factories[4] and their population, the number agents estimated as 500. So, we used 500 agents for both societies. In systems with high mortality rate α, was calculated so that in 10 years it reaches 1% for low life expectancy. Moreover, in Julfa we used numbers based on reported customary interest rate ($\approx 10\% \rightarrow (1/1.1) \approx 90\%$) [12]. Each agent has a finite time horizon (6 years) for calculating his utility function. The mortality rates, their functions, and reproduction rates for the two societies are obtained from [2, 7, 10, 13].

Table 4. Simulation parameters

Name	Description	Distribution	Value(s)
Discount Factor	Low Mortality Rate	Normal	(0.9, 0.033)
	High Mortality Rate	(μ, σ)	(0.63, 0.12)
Years	Constant	6	
Revenue	Both local and Masters	Uniform	(0.05, 0.1)
Population	Mature population (Plus kids for closed system)	Constant	500
Potential cheater rate	Chance of being a potential cheater	Constant	0.5
Proportion to Fire	Fired per run for bad performance (no adjudication process)	Constant	0.004
Revenue Extent	Linear function of skill	Uniform	(0, 0.1)
Skill	Maximum attainable skill	Uniform	(0.5, 1)
Chance of Identifying Cheaters	By agents with direct link	Uniform	(0, 1)
	By masters in closed system	Beta	(1, 5)
	By masters in open system, discounted by 1% for disloyalty	Uniform	(0, 1)

Furthermore, based on the approximated ROR associated with EIC during 1710–1745, the average is 9.74[5]. In our model, we assume a minimum revenue can

---

[4] For a list of these factories in India see [19], Map 2 (p. 65).

[5] A detailed table is provided in [4], Table A.26 (p. 440).

be made by trade that merchants cannot manipulate. Then, each agent starts with 100 units of money from master's capital, 10 units of money of his own capital for local trades. They have approximately 20 random connections with other agents that can observe and learn from. A new employee creates around 20 random connections to agents presented in the system; the connection is lost once a person leaves the society. Finally, the bonds are 50 units of money for agents with 1–5 years of experience, 100 for agents with 6–8 years of experience, and 150 for more experienced ones.

4   Simulation Results

In this section we discuss simulation results for 10 systems we considered. We used 30 different seeds for each system then averaged their results. Moreover, we assume each run reflects a year, and both systems used these institutions for around 150–200 years[6]. So, the number of runs in this simulation was bounded to 200 iterations. We gradually change attributes of EIC to get closer to Julfa to examine their effects. Based on these combinations we study the effectiveness of these systems in identifying and firing cheaters, reducing the percentage of the cheaters, improving the skill of people, and making more profits. It is worth mentioning that we did not add punishment compensations when calculating income, because it makes it hard to identify the real reason for system's profitability. In Table 5 attributes of these societies are presented (because punishment is a function of having adjudication process plus the contract form, we did not include it in this table). Each societal configuration is denoted by a Roman number, e.g., I indicates a closed society facing high mortality rate without commenda and adjudication process.

Table 5. System setups

Attributes	EIC	I	II	III	IV	V	VI	VII	VIII	Julfa
Commenda	✗	✗	✗	✗	✓	✗	✗	✓	✓	✓
Open	✓	✗	✗	✗	✗	✓	✓	✓	✓	✗
Adjudication	✗	✗	✗	✓	✗	✗	✓	✗	✓	✓
Mortality Rate	H	H	L	L	L	L	L	L	L	L

Now, we discuss the results of simulation runs which are indicated in Fig. 2. The x-axis of this figure represents number of years from system establishment and the y-axis indicates percentage of cheaters in society (for Fig. 2a-2f). Moreover, comparisons between EIC and Julfa (Fig. 2g) and two systems with unique behaviour (Fig. 2h) are represented for further discussion. The aforementioned

---

[6] EIC legalised local trades for agents in late 17th and early 18th AD and Julfans were active for less than 200 years.

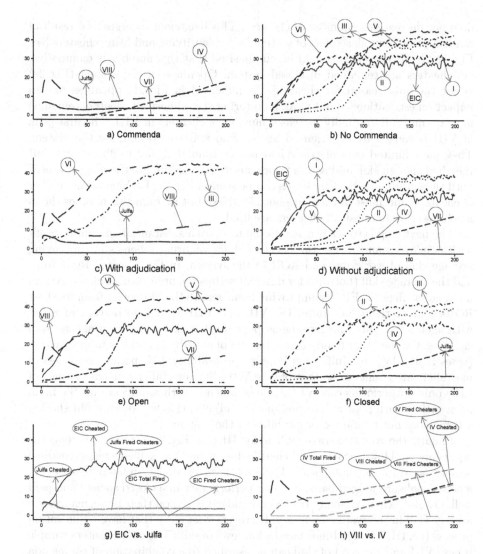

Fig. 2. Percentage of fired and cheater members of society, x-axis is number of years and y-axis is percentage of cheaters in society for (a–f). Percentage of cheaters, fired agents, and fired cheaters present for selected societies in (g–h).

figure (Fig. 2g–2h) includes the percentage of cheaters, fired cheaters, and total fired agents. As can be seen, there are fewer cheaters in systems run by commenda (Fig. 2a) than those with no commenda (Fig. 2b), that indicates impact of this profit sharing on agents behaviour. With or without adjudication (Fig. 2c–2d) does not decrease the number of cheaters except for VII. Moreover, as indicated in Fig. 2h it would create an increasing cheating trend in IV (which is like Julfa except with adjudication). Furthermore, closedness of workforce society (Fig. 2f) does not decrease the number of cheaters. This behaviour emerges as a result of random priors, but closedness of system helps identifying and firing cheaters (see Fig. 2g–2h). However, it should be emphasised that this number is cumulative, i.e. cheaters are remained in closed system. Openness of the system (Fig. 2e) is not the only reason for cheating. As indicated in Fig. 2h, openness has an impact on estimations about weak monitoring (i.e. almost all cheaters remained in next run) and gradually increases number of cheaters in VIII. The first peak in VIII is caused by experienced agents who started working for the system. They have limited capital (they had not accumulated any profit before), but they had enough skill and access to organisation's capital. So, these agents cheat until they gradually die. Finally, as can be seen in Fig. 2g, EIC has a big number of cheaters, and most of them are not identified; but in Julfa this number shows much lower and almost all cheaters are fired.

The next step is to see if it is rational to share a substantial amount of profit with employees and assess the effect of different firing schemes on improving average skill of workforce and ROR in the system. In Fig. 3 sorted ROR (top) and the average skill (bottom) for different setups are presented. A closed system has a good effect for EIC by improving managers ROR. Moreover, from five best RORs four of them, i.e. Julfa, IV, VII, and VIII shared 30 percent of profit with agents. So, this sharing scheme pays itself back by deterring agents from cheating. On the other hand, a combination of closedness and low mortality rate (cases II, III, IV, and Julfa) can improve profitability. EIC policy, regardless of mortality rate is inferior so that of case V (i.e. low mortality rate counterpart of EIC) only outperforms case VI (i.e. no commenda with adjudication). So, in an open society with poor monitoring, having adjudication without a profit sharing scheme does not guarantee profitability of the system.

Finally, the worst average skill is for III (see Fig. 3 bottom), wherein, the agents are paid low, cheated, and identified soon, and low-skilled agents remained as long as they did not cheat. The best level of skill is related to case IV, where people are judged based on their performance in a closed society and paid well. Overall, when company traders are judged based on their performance, the average skill in the system increases. However, most cases that have adjudication process (i.e. III, VI, and Julfa) faced a low level of skill. The only counter example is case VIII and the level of skill can be ascribed to a combination of commenda and openness, i.e. cheaters are present in the system and gain more skill. Finally, EIC was far better in improving skill of agents, especially if we consider its low mortality rate counterpart (V). Using the Wilcoxon Test we learn that there is not any significant difference among RORs of II, IV, VII, VIII, and Julfa (commenda payments and EIC with low mortality rate and closed workforce). These systems outperform other societies in profitability. Moreover, RORs of I, V, and VI do not indicate any significant difference (in an open workforce society adjudication process is not helpful). Average skill in IV and V (EIC with low mortality rate) dominates all other societies, and III shows the lowest skill level across all other societies. With these insights in mind, in the following section we discuss these results and their implications, before providing pointers towards future work.

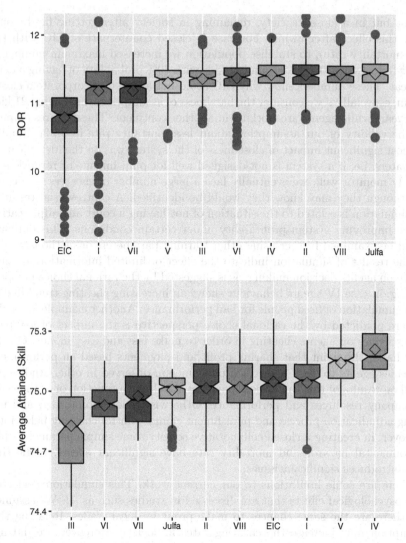

Fig. 3. ROR (top) and average skill (bottom) for different system settings.

5   Discussion

This study sheds some lights on what happened in two historical societies, namely EIC and Julfa. The simulation inspired by Greif's work [8] uses an incomplete information game aimed to investigate effects of some institutional attributes of EIC and Julfa. The results suggest that it is rational to share a significant amount of profit and then punish cheaters based on the revealed cheating. This scheme increases profitability of the system without other auxiliary means, i.e. adjudication process or monitoring. Moreover, a combination of no adjudication process and commenda may persuade agents to avoid cheating at first but in a closed society, remaining in society after getting fired would invert this effect after awhile. For case I (closed counterpart of EIC with the same mortality rate), to stabilise population we increased maximum number of agents from 1.4 to 10.4, i.e. around 21 kids with 70% probability of having a child per year. These numbers show why EIC could not afford to incorporate a closed system, especially if we consider the harshness of assumptions, i.e. having 21 kids in 30 years while agents are working in another continent. These figures emphasise the validity of our assumption about less mortality rate in Julfa. Finally, the most significant impact of closedness of the system was on the identification of cheaters, i.e. if a system is not designed well for punishments or rewards and we only monitor well, we eventually face a large number of cheaters in society, even though they may know they would be identified. A controversial result of this simulation is related to the situation of not having a court and adjudication chance improving system profitability under certain conditions. This outcome should be examined further using other learning parameters or methods.

The results of simulation indicate the effect of limited information about a system on agents decision making, as is suggested by the rational choice perspective, e.g. in case IV agents behaviour shows an increasing cheating trend due to the accumulation of fired people for bad performance. Another example of results that are predicted by the rational choice perspective is the impact of low payment schemes on agents cheating in order to make fast and easy money. On the other hand, the point that sharing profit and payments based on performance persuades agents to work better is a phenomenon observed in other studies [9]. Based on results of this simulation, payment should be a function of both access to company resources and performance. Otherwise, good monitoring, and not having adjudication process and punishment cannot control cheating behaviour. Moreover, in creating a closed collaborative society some simple parameters like environmental hazards and mortality rate have significant effects. Neglecting them introduces significant issues.

There are some limitations to our current work. This simulation neglected some psychological effects that are discussed in studies such as [1]. We assumed that there are the same chances to make profit by local trades. Relaxing this assumption may increase the cheating rates in society. Moreover, we did not consider certain aspects in this study such as mimicking other participants' behaviour, consequences of living in a system with a high proportion of cheaters, or punished cheaters. For future work, we will consider effects of informal apprenticeship and sharing information about opportunities in closed systems and the impact of payment on the loyalty of agents in an open system.

References

1. Adams, J.S.: Inequity in social exchange. Adv. Exp. Soc. Psychol. **2**, 267–299 (1965)
2. Aslanian, S.D.: From the Indian Ocean to the Mediterranean: Circulation and the Global Trade Networks of Armenian Merchants from New Julfa/Isfahan, 1605–1747. Ph.D. thesis, Columbia University (2007)

3. Chaudhuri, K.N.: The English East India Company: The Study of an Early Joint-stock Company 1600–1640. Frank Cass & Co Ltd., London (1965)
4. Chaudhuri, K.N.: The Trading World of Asia and the English East India Company: 1660–1760. Cambridge University Press, Cambridge (1978)
5. Erikson, E.: Between Monopoly and Free Trade: The English East India Company, 1600–1757. Princeton University Press, Princeton (2014)
6. Frantz, C., Purvis, M.K., Nowostawski, M.: Agent-based modeling of information transmission in early historic trading. Soc. Sci. Comput. Rev. **32**(3), 393–416 (2014)
7. Frolkis, V.V.: Experimental life prolongation. In: Frolkis, V.V. (ed.) Aging and Life-Prolonging Processes, pp. 306–340. Springer, Vienna (1982). https://doi.org/10.1007/978-3-7091-8649-7_14
8. Greif, A.: Contract enforceability and economic institutions in early trade: The Maghribi traders' coalition. The American economic review **83**, 525–548 (1993)
9. Haubrich, J.G.: Risk aversion, performance pay, and the principal-agent problem. J. Polit. Econ. **102**(2), 258–276 (1994)
10. Hejeebu, S.: Microeconomic investigations of the English East India Company. Ph.D. thesis, University of Iowa (2000)
11. Hejeebu, S.: Contract enforcement in the English East India Company. J. Econ. Hist. **65**(2), 496–523 (2005)
12. Herzig, E.M.: The Armenian Merchants of New Julfa, Isfahan: A study in pre-modern Asian trade. Ph.D. thesis, D. Phil., Oxford (1991)
13. Hollingsworth, T.H.: A demographic study of the British ducal families. Popul. Stud. **11**(1), 4–26 (1957)
14. Holmstrom, B., Milgrom, P.: Multitask principal-agent analyses: incentive contracts, asset ownership, and job design. J. Law Econ. Organ. **7**, 24–52 (1991)
15. Marshall, P.J.: East Indian Fortunes: The British in Bengal in the Eighteenth Century. Oxford University Press, Oxford (1976)
16. Myerson, R.B.: Optimal coordination mechanisms in generalized principal-agent problems. J. Math. Econ. **10**(1), 67–81 (1982)
17. North, D.C.: Institutional Change and Economic Performance. Cambridge University Press, New York (1990)
18. Plato, Jowett, B.: Apology. public domain. Champaign, Ill : Project Gutenberg. (nd)
19. Robins, N.: The Corporation that Changed the World: How the East India Company Shaped the Modern Multinational. Pluto Press, Chicago (2017)
20. Seth, V.K.: The East India Company-a case study in corporate governance. Glob. Bus. Rev. **13**(2), 221–238 (2012)

Indirect Influence Manipulation with Partial Observability

James Archbold[(✉)] and Nathan Griffiths

University of Warwick, Coventry, UK
{james.archbold,Nathan.Griffiths}@warwick.ac.uk

Abstract. The propagation of concepts through a population of agents can be modelled as a cascade of influence spread from an initial set of individuals. In real-world environments there may be many concepts spreading and interacting, and we may not be able to directly control the target concept we wish to manipulate, requiring indirect manipulation through a secondary controllable concept. Previous work on influence spread typically assumes that we have full knowledge of a network, which may not be the case. In this paper, we investigate indirect influence manipulation when we can only observe a sample of the full network. We propose a heuristic, known as Target Degree, for selecting seed nodes for a secondary controllable concept that uses the limited information available in a partially observable environment to indirectly manipulate the target concept. Target degree is shown to be effective in synthetic small-world networks and in real-world networks when the controllable concept is introduced after the target concept.

Keywords: Influence spread · Social networks · Information diffusion

1 Introduction

In many environments, strategies, concepts or infections may spread within a population. The nature of propagation is determined by the interactions between individuals. Populations of autonomous entities are complex systems, meaning that the net effects of propagation are hard to predict or influence, despite being due to individual behaviour. Such propagation is a form of influence spread, which can be modelled as a cascade from a set of initial individual agents [8]. The propagation of concepts between agents can affect individual behaviour, which in turn can affect the behaviour of the overall system. Influence spread techniques have applications in epidemiology, marketing and behavioural science, and can involve an agent-based simulation of a real-world problem. Understanding concept propagation aids in the identification of influential individuals, who can help or hinder a concept's spread.

Several models have been developed to characterise influence spread [4], along with techniques to maximise spread [3]. A population can be represented as a network, through which concepts spread. Nodes represent individuals and edges

© Springer Nature Switzerland AG 2019
P. Davidsson and H. Verhagen (Eds.): MABS 2018, LNAI 11463, pp. 32–44, 2019.
https://doi.org/10.1007/978-3-030-22270-3_3

represent the influence that exists between pairs of individuals. Concept spread is maximised through the strategic selection of a set of nodes, known as the seed set, to begin a cascade through the network. Selecting an effective seed set has been the focus of much work. Multi-concept models typically assume that concepts *block* each other, preventing a node from activating multiple concepts simultaneously [6]. However, in the real-world an individual may have many concepts active, which may interact and affect how concepts spread.

For example, consider how political beliefs are developed. The news stories and opinion articles that a person reads, and decides are reputable, will affect the political affiliation they are likely to adopt. Furthermore, this will affect the types of articles and opinions that they share with those within their social circle. Similarly, in epidemiology, a disease may cause symptoms in an individual that encourages the spread of other diseases.

If concepts interact, we can consider how to indirectly affect the spread of a concept that cannot be directly controlled. A common example of this is inoculation and education to limit the spread of a disease, but we could also promote particular news stories to improve the spread of a particular political opinion, or lower the sales of a product through competing products. In all these cases, the target concept cannot be controlled directly and so we use another controllable concept to boost or inhibit the spread of the target concept.

Recent work has utilised concept interaction to indirectly affect the spread of a target concept that cannot be directly controlled. Liontis and Pitorua proposed the MoBoo heuristic, which evaluates the possible gain from selecting a node [10]. Archbold and Griffiths proposed the Maximum Probable Gain (MPG) heuristic to select seeds for a secondary controllable concept to indirectly affect the spread of the target concept [2].

Previous work assumes that we have knowledge of the entire network, but mapping real-world social networks is expensive and is often infeasible. Typically, when working with real-world networks, only a small sample can be observed, which may not be representative and limits the information known about the network. Thus, we wish to effectively manipulate influence within a network when we can only observe a sample of that network to inform our decisions.

In this paper, we study the problem of indirect influence manipulation when we have only partial network information. We present a heuristic to select a seed set for a controllable concept from a small sample of a full network, known as Target Degree, and compare it to random selection, degree-based selection, single discount, degree discount, MPG and MoBoo.

2   Related Work

Several influence propagation models have been proposed in the literature [8]. Two of the most widely discussed are the *Independent Cascade Model* (ICM) and the *Linear Threshold Model* (LTM). The ICM treats influence as particle diffusion, with each node given a single chance, on activation, to activate a concept on each inactive neighbour, with some probability, p [4]. The LTM emulates social peer pressure, with every active neighbour of a node being considered [8]. Each node v has a threshold θ_v, and if the sum of the weights of v's active neighbours exceeds θ_v, then v becomes active.

The problem of influence maximisation has been widely studied, resulting in many different approaches. A basic hill-climbing approach that selects the node that provides the largest incremental increase to the performance of the current seed set can be effective [5], but is typically intractable in practice. Chen *et al.* proposed the Degree Discount heuristic for the ICM, which accounts for existing activations by ranking nodes by degree and decrementing that degree when a node's neighbours are selected to be seeds [3]. Degree Discount has been shown to be both effective and tractable.

In real-world environments, there may be many concepts spreading through a population. Thus, recent work has considered multiple influence cascades, but typically assumes that cascades are blocking, preventing a node from activating multiple concepts [7]. If concepts are not blocking, then their interactions must be considered. Sanz *et al.* developed a multi-layer network model in which each concept spreads on a separate layer, but nodes can have multiple concepts active, and concepts can interact [12]. Through interaction a concept can *boost* or *inhibit* the spread of another concept. Considering these interactions has resulted in new influence maximisation strategies [1].

Liontis and Pitoura developed the MoBoo algorithm for indirectly boosting the spread of a concept [10]. Nodes are selected to have an increased probability to spread the target concept. MoBoo constructs a series of trees from nodes with the target concept active, and selects nodes based on how many trees they appear in and the number of child nodes they have in each tree. Concept interaction introduces the ability to contain rumours, by indirectly limiting the spread of a concept [9]. Existing approaches to rumour containment also often assume that concepts block, and attempt to partition the network and make traversal difficult [11]. However, this approach becomes less effective when concept, and therefore path, blocking can not be guaranteed. The MPG heuristic uses local exploration, identifying those nodes that are likely to activate the target concept [2]. These nodes also have their neighbourhood explored, to determine their expected gain. MPG selects nodes with both high activation probability and high expected gain, for the controllable concept's seed set.

There has been relatively little work that considers partial observability in the context of influence spread. Partially observable Markov decision process planners [14] and greedy, oracle-based, algorithms [13] have been used to account for uncertainty when directly maximising influence. However, these methods only consider single concepts, rather than multiple interacting concepts.

3 Concept Interaction

In this paper, we consider the indirect influence maximisation problem and the indirect influence limitation problem, which require selecting a seed set of size k for a controllable concept with the aim of affecting the spread of a target concept. In the indirect influence maximisation problem, we aim to increase the spread of the target concept and in the indirect influence limitation problem, we aim to minimise the spread of the target concept. Both problems assume that concepts interact and affect each other's spread, which we model in a similar way to Sanz *et al.*'s approach for two interacting concepts [12].

We model a set of agents as a network, where nodes represent individual agents and edges represent a connection that allows for influence to be exerted. When two agents interact, influence is sent by the *infector* to the *receiver* and the receiver will potentially activate a particular concept that is active on the infector. We denote the strength of the influence exerted by node v on node u with respect to concept c as $I_{v,u}(c)$. Any value $I_{v,u}(c) > 0$ means that v has some influence over u, represented as an edge in a network.

The relationship between two concepts is defined by the effect that one has on the other's ability to spread, represented as a numerical value. The variable $CR(c, c')$ describes the effect that c' has on the ability of c to spread when present on the infector or receiver. In this paper, we assume that c' affects concept spread in the same way, regardless of whether it is active on the infector or receiver.

We assume that $CR(c, c') \in [0, \infty)$ is a feature of the environment. If $CR(c, c') < 1$ then c' is inhibiting and decreases the chance of c to spread, and if $CR(c, c') > 1$ then c' is boosting and increases the chance of c to spread. If $CR(c, c') = 1$ then c' has no effect on the ability of c to spread. $CR(c, c')$ is used to define the contextual influence that v can exert on u with respect to concept c, $CI_{v,u}(c)$, which accounts for concept relationships as follows:

$$CI_{v,u}(c) = \begin{cases} I_{v,u}(c) & \text{if } c' \text{ is not active on either } v \text{ or } u \\ I_{v,u}(c) * CR(c, c') & \text{if } c' \text{ is active on either } v \text{ or } u \\ I_{v,u}(c) * CR(c, c')^2 & \text{if } c' \text{ is active on both } v \text{ and } u. \end{cases} \tag{1}$$

Note that the effect of c' is compounded when it is active on both the infector and receiver, in the same way that individuals can be more easily influenced by people who they perceive as similar to themselves.

To model concept propagation, we adapt the ICM to allow for multiple simultaneous cascades. Cascades proceed in rounds, with the nodes in each concept's seed set activating that concept in round 0. In each subsequent round, nodes that activated a concept in the previous round have a chance to activate that concept on each of their neighbours. This continues until there are no new activations for any concept. Activations happen simultaneously, and so the contextual influence can only be affected by concepts active before the current round. In this model, we use $I_{v,u}(c)$ as the chance of node v successfully activating c on node u.

4   Target Degree

We wish to indirectly manipulate the spread of a target concept in an environment where we are only able to observe a small sample of a network. Previous heuristics assume full knowledge of the network, and may require in-depth exploration of a node's neighbourhood in order to select a seed set for the controllable concept. However, such analysis is impractical when only a sample can be observed. Sampling a node does not guarantee that all edges of the node are observed, making degree-based selection unreliable. Thus, a node's observable, explorable, neighbourhood may not be representative of the influence it can exert in the full network, and so we require a new method of seed selection.

We propose the **Target Degree** (TD) heuristic, which ranks nodes by the number of neighbours with the target concept active. If a node is in the observable sample, we assume that we know whether it has the target concept active. If a node with the target concept active has unobserved edges, activating the controllable concept on that node will not only affect the spread of the target concept in the observable area, but also increase the chance of interacting with the target concept in the unobserved network. A node with the target concept active is likely to have neighbours with the target concept active or is likely to spread the target concept to its neighbours. Without full network knowledge, we focus on the immediate benefits and activate the controllable concept on nodes that either have the target concept active or have many neighbours with the target concept active.

As such, for TD, we create two ranked lists, L_t and $L_{\neg t}$, of nodes with the target concept active and nodes without the target concept active respectively. In each list, nodes are ranked based on the number of neighbours they have with the target concept active, in descending order. We then append $L_{\neg t}$ to end of L_t to create the combined list, L. For a seed set of size k, we select the first k elements of list L. TD can be efficiently calculated and does not require additional calculations after the selection of individual seed nodes, as is the case with several existing heuristics such as degree discount, MPG and MoBoo. We evaluate TD against the following heuristics.

Degree-Based Selection. Degree-based selection is a simple heuristic, that is cheap to compute and has been shown to be effective [8]. In degree-based selection, the k nodes with the highest degree are selected as the seed set.

Single Discount. This heuristic accounts for the fact that a node selected to be in the seed set cannot be activated by its neighbours, meaning that the neighbours of a selected seed node suffer a decrease in non-active neighbours that can potentially be activated. In single discount, the highest degree node is selected, and the degree of its neighbours is lowered by 1. This process is repeated until the full seed set is selected [3].

Degree Discount. Selecting a node as a seed lowers the expected gain of its neighbours, and increases the chance its neighbours may be activated in the first round. Degree discount therefore weights a node's degree based on the number of its neighbours previously selected to be seed nodes. Nodes are ranked by degree, and when a node is selected its neighbours have their degree set to $d_v - 2t_v - (d_v - t_v) * t_v * p$, where d_v is the original degree, t_v is the number of neighbours in the seed set and p is the probability of infection. The full derivation of this calculation can be found in [3].

Table 1. Experimental parameters.

Parameter	Values
Proportion of network sample (nodes) (SN)	0.1, 0.2, 0.3
Sampling Methods (SM)	Snowball, MHDA
Seed set size (SS)	10, 25, 50, 100, 250, 500
CR function values for the controllable concept	0, 0.2, 0.4, 0.6, 0.8, 1.2, 1.4, 1.6, 1.8, 2
Burn-in time for the controllable concept (BI)	0, 2, 5

MoBoo. In this heuristic, nodes are evaluated based on their expected gain if they were to be selected as a boosting node. Using the two most probable independent paths for the target concept to reach a node v, the activation probability $ap(v)$ is calculated as the probability that the target concept reaches v from one or both of the paths. The gain for a node, v, is then calculated as:

$$g(v) = \sum_{u \in Out(v)} \left(\frac{p'_{v,u}}{p_{v,u}} - 1 \right) \sum_{w \text{ descendant of } u} ap(w)$$

where $Out(v)$ is the set of nodes that are the children of v in either path, $p_{v,u}$ is the probability of the concept spreading from node v to u and $p'_{v,u} = p_{v,u} + b$, with b being the improvement gained by a node being a boosting node. Each round, the node with the highest gain is chosen until we have the desired number of nodes. Full details of MoBoo can be found in [10].

MPG. This heuristic also calculates the activation probability and expected gain of each node. However, MPG limits its exploration to paths with an influence value higher than a set threshold, θ. The influence value, I_P, of a path $P = \{v_1 \rightarrow \ldots \rightarrow v_n\}$ with respect to target concept t, is calculated as the product of all $CI_{v_i,v_{i+1}}(t)$ values in the path.

The most influential path to node u from node v with respect to t is defined as $MIP(v, u) = \text{argmax}_{P \in AP_{v,u}}(I_P)$, where $AP_{v,u}$ is the set of all paths that start with v and end in u. The influence value of $MIP(v, u)$ is denoted as $I_{MIP(v,u)}$, and an influence value less than θ is treated as 0. Thus, the influence received from v by u, $IR(v, u)$ is set to $I_{MIP(v,u)}$ or to 0 if $I_{MIP(v,u)} < \theta$.

The activation probability of node u, $ap(u)$, is defined as the sum of all $IR(v, u)$ values where v is actively spreading the target concept. In the case of the ICM, this means that v was activated in the previous cascade round. The expected gain of u, $E(u)$, is the sum of all $IR(u, w)$ values where w is a node without the target concept active. The weighted expected gain, $WE(u)$, for node u is defined as $WE(u) = E(u) \times ap(u)$. The node with the highest $WE(u)$ value is selected, and $WE(v)$ is recalculated for unselected nodes, until the seed set reaches its desired size. Full details can be found in [2].

Table 2. Characteristics of the real-world networks used for evaluation.

Network	Nodes	Edges	Avg. degree	Avg. clustering coefficient	Num. of triangles	Diameter
CA-CondMat (CM)	23133	93497	4.04	0.6334	173361	14
cit-HepPh (HP)	34546	421578	12.2	0.2848	1276868	12
DBLP (DB)	317080	1049866	3.31	0.6324	2224385	21

5   Experimental Approach

To simulate partial observability, we select controllable concept seeds from an observable subset of nodes in a network, sampled through either snowball sampling or through a Metropolis Hasting random walk with Delayed Acceptance (MHDA). Snowball sampling maintains the local structure of an area in the network, while MHDA produces a sample with characteristics, such as degree distribution, more in line with those of the full network, but at the expense of maintaining local structure. We consider various sampling proportions to represent varying degrees of observability, as listed in Table 1.

For each combination of parameters in Table 1, we perform 50 simulations for each of the heuristics described in Sect. 4 along with random selection to act as a baseline. We perform two tailed t-tests between heuristics to test for statistical significance. The controllable concept is introduced after a fixed number of time steps, known as the burn-in time. This is kept low, as high burn-in times result in indirect influence manipulation being ineffective [2]. The target concept is introduced at time step 0, and its seed set is randomly selected from the full network. Simulations are performed using the ICM, and each concept has a probability of spreading to a neighbour of $I_{v,u}(c) = 0.1$.

In this paper, we consider a selection of representative networks. Synthetic small-world networks, with a size of 100000 nodes and a clustering exponent of 0.75, are generated using the Kleinberg small world generator in the JUNG graph framework[1]. Synthetic scale-free networks with 100000 nodes are constructed using the Barabási-Albert generator provided in JUNG, which begins with a set of unconnected nodes, 10 in this case, and introduces a new node each evolution step. The new node gains a number of edges, 4 in this case, connected to existing nodes using preferential attachment. A number of real-world networks[2] are used, based on datasets from the Stanford SNAP project[3], as listed in Table 2.

For the small-world, scale-free, and DB real-world networks we use seed set sizes of $100, 250, 500$. Since the observable samples of the CM and HP networks often contain less than 7500 nodes, we use the seed set sizes of $10, 25, 50$ to prevent the seed set from a majority of the sample.

---

[1] http://jung.sourceforge.net/.

[2] These networks are samples of full social networks, but for the purposes of this paper we treat them as the complete network.

[3] http://snap.stanford.edu/data/index.html.

Table 3. Average infections for the target concept in networks with $SN = 0.2$, $SS = 250$ and $BI = 0$, with standard deviation in brackets, and the best performing heuristic in bold.

Network type	Sampling method	CR value	Target degree	MPG	MoBoo	Degree discount	Single discount	Degree
SW	MHDA	0	**494.14** **(32.82)**	533.86 (36.17)	554.88 (37.13)	553.72 (37.01)	553.66 (37.01)	554.44 (37.49)
SW	Snow	0	**489.96** **(33.12)**	525.62 (35.53)	555.8 (37.3)	553.02 (37.83)	553.08 (37.86)	553.78 (37.5)
SW	MHDA	2	**651.82** **(45.96)**	635.76 (43.58)	611.2 (44.14)	562.48 (37.98)	562.48 (37.98)	562.58 (38.92)
SW	Snow	2	**657.52** **(42.55)**	603.72 (38.15)	624.98 (40.45)	569.88 (39.09)	569.14 (39.31)	569.3 (39.99)
SF	MHDA	0	7565.02 (1676.26)	6852.68 (1420.88)	6887.36 (1091.64)	6827.02 (1402.93)	**6805.14** **(1392.88)**	6866.82 (1510.26)
SF	Snow	0	2613.22 (754.62)	1724.64 (343.79)	10480 (2114.67)	1420.98 (238.4)	1403.96 (245.64)	**1402.9** **(298.49)**
SF	MHDA	2	33673.52 (756.82)	35075.02 (852.79)	35230.6 (891.54)	35495.22 (893.7)	35528.9 (883.2)	**35588.1** **(872.15)**
SF	Snow	2	37017.62 (765.79)	39252.76 (634.52)	38806.04 (659.84)	40675.74 (534.25)	**40687.26** **(582.2)**	40684.02 (511.53)

6   Results

To begin, we discuss the synthetic networks. Results for the synthetic small-world and scale-free networks can be seen in Table 3, for when the burn-in time is 0. In general, the sampling proportion and seed set size only impact the magnitude of the results, but not the relative performance, and so we do not discuss them further, in regards to the synthetic networks.

As can be seen in Table 3, we see that in small-world networks with a burn-in of 0, TD statistically significantly outperforms ($p < 0.01$) all other heuristics for each sampling proportion, sampling method and seed set size for both inhibiting and boosting the target concept. Comparatively, in scale-free networks we see that degree-based heuristics perform best. In general, we see that TD is the worst performing heuristic in scale-free networks, particularly when attempting to inhibit the target concept. When attempting to boost the target concept, the difference in performance between all heuristics is relatively small and, in general, not statistically significant.

As the burn-in time increases, for both small-world and scale-free networks, the heuristics begin to perform at the same level. Table 4 shows the two different patterns of performance we see as the burn-in time increases. In small-world networks, we see that only TD's performance significantly changes as the burn-in time increases to 2, but it continues to outperform the other heuristics and then, at the highest burn-in time, there is no statistically significant difference between the heuristics. In snowball sampled scale-free networks we see a similar pattern,

Table 4. Average infections for the target concept in networks with $SN = 0.2$, $SS = 250$, $CR = 0$ and $SM = MHDA$, with standard deviation in brackets, and the best performing heuristic in bold.

Network type	Burn-in time	Target degree	MPG	MoBoo	Degree discount	Single discount	Degree
SW	2	**541.2** (**34.24**)	551.92 (36.09)	551.96 (36.37)	557.0 (37.82)	557.0 (37.82)	557.38 (37.93)
SW	5	**555.94** (**37.53**)	556.54 (37.63)	556.46 (37.46)	557.7 (38)	557.7 (38)	557.7 (38)
SF	2	**8390.06** (**1052.69**)	11630.76 (1288.63)	11755.16 (1163.19)	11738.56 (1307.4)	11751.9 (1307.14)	11697.38 (1459.65)
SF	5	**16192.8** (**1007.95**)	16786.46 (645.81)	17034.88 (760.98)	16556.06 (716.85)	16558.16 (718.6)	16554.48 (760.27)

in that all heuristics converge to similar performance as the burn-in increases, and the best performing heuristic does not change. For MHDA sampled scale-free networks, as seen in Table 4, TD's relative performance improves as the burn-in time increases. At a burn-in time of 2, TD is the best performing heuristic by a significant margin. At a burn-in time of 5, the target concept has performed the majority of its spreading, and so manipulating the concept at that point will yield minimal results, meaning that there is no significant difference between the heuristics.

Overall, when considering synthetic networks, we see that TD is the best choice for small-world networks, regardless of sampling method. We also see that TD is less affected by burn-in time than other heuristics, which allows it to perform well in MHDA sampled scale-free networks. Thus, if we can control the sampling method of a network, TD becomes a strong choice for manipulating the spread of a target concept.

Considering real-world networks, we see that the use of snowball sampling results in a similar performance to that seen in the scale-free synthetic networks. Thus, due to space limitations, we focus on the MHDA samples. Figures 1 and 2 show the difference in performance for a subset of heuristics at different burn-in times, for boosting and inhibiting the target concept respectively. We omit degree-based selection and single discount as they perform similarly to degree discount in all cases. MoBoo is omitted as it performs consistently poorly at inhibition and is comparable to MPG at boosting. Both figures are for the CM network, with the HP network exhibiting similar results.

Figure 1 shows that, as the burn-in increases, TD improves its performance and outperforms the other heuristics, as in the scale-free networks. In Fig. 2, TD is the best performing heuristic when the CR value and burn-in time is low, and than similarly improves as the burn-in time increases.

This resistance to burn-in time is particularly advantageous for real-world applications, where it can be difficult to introduce a controllable concept to a network at the exact same time as the target concept.

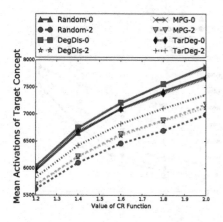
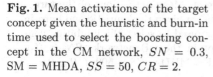
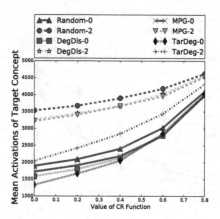

Fig. 1. Mean activations of the target concept given the heuristic and burn-in time used to select the boosting concept in the CM network, $SN = 0.3$, SM = MHDA, $SS = 50$, $CR = 2$.

Fig. 2. Mean activations of the target concept given the heuristic and burn-in time used to select the inhibiting concept in the CM network, $SN = 0.3$, SM = MHDA, $SS = 50$, $CR = 0$.

In the DB network, Fig. 3 shows that, when inhibiting the target concept from a MHDA sample, increasing the burn-in time increases TD's performance. However, increasing the sampling proportion, as in Fig. 4, causes MPG to maintain superior performance at higher burn-in times. DB is the sparsest network, with the highest diameter, meaning that most nodes have few local connections and are not closely connected to the rest of the network. As such, at higher burn-in times, it is less likely for unobserved nodes to affect the observed sample. Increasing the sampling proportion further removes the few unobserved connections that may exist, which in turn can improve the performance of exploration. This also occurs when boosting the target concept, although TD is never the best performing heuristic in this case.

Overall, in real-world networks, we see that increasing the burn-in time generally improves the comparative performance of TD to a point, after which every heuristic performs at a similar level. At higher burn-in times, there is a higher chance of observed nodes having activated the target concept from an unobserved node. By selecting these nodes, TD is more likely to influence the unobserved network and is more likely to interact with the target concept.

Furthermore, we see that MHDA sampling allows TD to perform better than snowball sampling. Snowball sampling is assumed to be capable of finding all edges of a node. As such, we perfectly sample a local area of the network. This means that, compared to the random walk approach of MHDA sampling, there are no unobserved edges. In an observed sample with no unobserved edges, in-depth path prediction is more reliable. When MHDA sampling is used, the number of unobserved edges increases and makes path prediction less effective. A node with the target concept active may have been activated by a neighbour in the unobserved part of the network, meaning that selecting these types of nodes

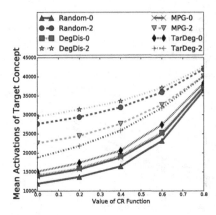 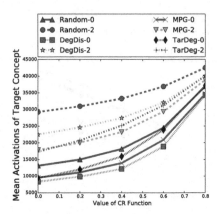

Fig. 3. Mean activations of the target concept given the heuristic and burn-in time used to select the inhibiting concept in the DB network, $SN = 0.1$, SM = MHDA, $SS = 500$, $CR = 0$.

Fig. 4. Mean activations of the target concept given the heuristic and burn-in time used to select the inhibiting concept in the DB network, $SN = 0.3$, SM = MHDA, $SS = 500$, $CR = 0$.

increases the chance for the controllable concept to affect the target concept in the unobserved area of the network.

Finally, we see a distinction between the synthetic small-world networks and the other networks observed. It is only in the synthetic small-world networks that TD outperforms all other heuristics in every environment. The presence of scale-free properties in the other networks means that degree-based heuristics are favoured in most cases, particularly in snowball samples. This, combined with TDs improved performance in MHDA samples, implies that TD performs better when there is a higher number of unobserved edges.

7   Conclusions and Future Work

In this work, we discuss the problem of indirectly manipulating the spread of a concept through concept interaction, when we do not have full network knowledge. We proposed the Target Degree (TD) heuristic that utilises minimal information and does not rely on in-depth network exploration, and compared its performance to several other heuristics for indirect influence manipulation.

TD was the best heuristic in the synthetic small-world networks, and is effective in scale-free networks sampled using MHDA with a burn-in time greater than 0. Otherwise, degree-based heuristics proved superior, and we see a similar result in the real-world networks studied. In nearly all cases, TD was the best performing heuristic at a burn-in time of 2 in MHDA samples, with the exception of the DB network, implying that TD requires denser networks to be effective. In real-world applications it may be impossible to introduce the controllable concept at the same time as the target concept, especially since we assume no control over the target concept, making TD a suitable option. Overall, for both synthetic and real-world networks, if the sampling method that determines which nodes can be observed can be selected, then TD may provide the best result.

TD performed poorly in snowball sampled networks, implying that it performs better with a higher number of unobserved edges. Sampling real-world networks is unlikely to be perfect, meaning that unobserved edges are more likely, providing further evidence of TDs suitability to real-world applications.

In future work, we wish to explore this problem in other influence spread models, including the Linear Threshold model and the Susceptible-Infected-Susceptible model. Furthermore, we will consider dynamic networks, where the observed sampled may lose or gain nodes and the unobserved network is updated as the concepts cascade through the network.

References

1. Archbold, J., Griffiths, N.: Maximising influence in non-blocking cascades of interacting concepts. In: Gaudou, B., Sichman, J.S. (eds.) MABS 2015. LNCS (LNAI), vol. 9568, pp. 173–187. Springer, Cham (2016). https://doi.org/10.1007/978-3-319-31447-1_12
2. Archbold, J., Griffiths, N.: Limiting concept spread in environments with interacting concepts. In: Proceedings of the 16th Conference on Autonomous Agents and MultiAgent Systems, pp. 1332–1340 (2017)
3. Chen, W., Wang, Y., Yang, S.: Efficient influence maximization in social networks. In: Proceedings of the 15th ACM SIGKDD International Conference on Knowledge Discovery and Data Mining, pp. 199–208 (2009)
4. Goldenberg, J., Libai, B., Muller, E.: Using complex systems analysis to advance marketing theory development. Acad. Mark. Sci. Rev. $9(3)$, 1–18 (2001)
5. Goyal, A., Lu, W., Lakshmanan, L.V.: Celf++: optimizing the greedy algorithm for influence maximization in social networks. In: Proceedings of the 20th ACM International Conference Companion on World Wide Web, pp. 47–48 (2011)
6. Goyal, S., Kearns, M.: Competitive contagion in networks. In: Proceedings of the 44th Annual ACM Symposium on Theory of Computing, pp. 759–774 (2012)
7. He, X., Song, G., Chen, W., Jiang, Q.: Influence blocking maximization in social networks under the competitive linear threshold model. In: Proceedings 12th SIAM International Conference on Data Mining, pp. 463–474 (2012)
8. Kempe, D., Kleinberg, J., Tardos, É.: Maximizing the spread of influence through a social network. In: Proceedings of the 9th ACM SIGKDD International Conference on Knowledge Discovery and Data Mining, pp. 137–146 (2003)
9. Li, S., Zhu, Y., Li, D., Kim, D., Huang, H.: Rumor restriction in online social networks. In: Proceedings of the 32nd IEEE International Performance Computing and Communications Conference, pp. 1–10 (2013)
10. Liontis, K., Pitoura, E.: Boosting nodes for improving the spread of influence. Preprint arXiv:1609.03478 (2016)
11. Masuda, N.: Immunization of networks with community structure. New J. Phys. $11(12)$, 123018 (2009)
12. Sanz, J., Xia, C.Y., Meloni, S., Moreno, Y.: Dynamics of interacting diseases. Phys. Rev. X $4(4)$, 041005 (2014)

13. Wilder, B., Yadav, A., Immorlica, N., Rice, E., Tambe, M.: Uncharted but not uninfluenced: influence maximization with an uncertain network. In: Proceedings of the 16th Conference on Autonomous Agents and MultiAgent Systems, pp. 1305–1313 (2017)
14. Yadav, A., Chan, H., Xin Jiang, A., Xu, H., Rice, E., Tambe, M.: Using social networks to aid homeless shelters: dynamic influence maximization under uncertainty. In: Proceedings of the 2016 International Conference on Autonomous Agents & Multiagent Systems, pp. 740–748 (2016)

Impact of Trust on Agent-Based Simulation for Supply Chains

André Jalbut and Jaime Simão Sichman[✉]

Laboratório de Técnicas Inteligentes (LTI), Escola Politécnica (EP),
Universidade de São Paulo (USP), São Paulo, Brazil
{andre.jalbut,jaime.sichman}@usp.br

Abstract. Companies in supply chains have a goal to optimize their productivity, and hence their profits. One way to study the behavior of these chains is to simulate them using a multi-agent approach. In this work, we propose an extension of a model used in the literature, called the *Beer Game*, by adding multiple agents in each of its levels to evaluate both the local and global performance of the suppliers. We use different agent profiles, based either on trust or on price. By enabling clients to ask supplier suggestions from their peers, we measure how these peers' suggestions and lies affect working capital and trust measures for different agent profiles.

1 Introduction

The main goal of every business is profit [6]. In the context of companies interacting in a supply chain (SC), partnerships based on trust can be more profitable than those based on supply and demand mechanisms. This statement is based on the observation that the greater the trust of a consumer in his suppliers, the greater the responsiveness of these, and therefore the greater the gain for SC [8].

Supply chains are defined as the set of organizations, activities, information and resources involved in the movement of a product or service from suppliers to consumers [14]. The interest in studying the management of these chains, supply chain management (SCM), has been increasing in order to obtain competitive advantages for the market through improvements in its processes [3]. Figure 1 [11] illustrates an example of SC.

On the other hand, trust may be defined as the predisposition of an agent to place himself in a vulnerable situation in relation to another hoping that this latter provides him with some benefit in return [13]. Since a SC is composed of individual firms collaborating to serve end-users, their effectiveness is highly dependent on trust between network partners [21].

In [19], the authors propose to simulate SCM with the aid of agent-based modeling (ABM), which allows chain performance to be evaluated under different organizational perspectives. In [4], researchers advocate the choice of ABM to simulate SCM because the latter is a physically distributed problem in which agents may consider both their own interests and the one of the entire chain;

© Springer Nature Switzerland AG 2019
P. Davidsson and H. Verhagen (Eds.): MABS 2018, LNAI 11463, pp. 45–58, 2019.
https://doi.org/10.1007/978-3-030-22270-3_4

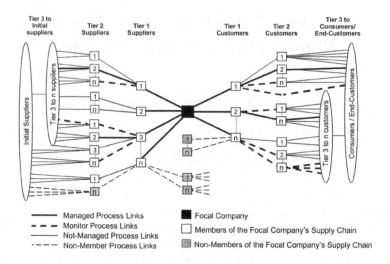

Fig. 1. Example of supply chain [11]

they also consider simulating SCM a highly complex problem, influenced by the interaction between several variables.

One way to model the behavior of the agents playing different roles in a SC is by using the structure proposed by the *Beer Game* (Sect. 2), a board game created within SCM and often cited in the literature. In [10], for example, the rules of this game are used in simulation to model the performance of the agents interacting in a SC.

The objective of this work is to analyze the impact of suggestions, lies and trust between entities inserted in the context of an SC modeled by the *Beer Game*, in particular simulating companies with different profiles.

2   Beer Game

The *Beer Game* is a board game designed by Forrester [5] to understand SCMs. In this game, teams of 4 players compete with each other; a team represents a supply chain and each team member plays one role, corresponding to four levels of the SC: factory, distributor, wholesaler and retailer. The objective of each team is to manage the stock in face of unknown external demand, trying to minimize the cumulative costs in the sum of the levels of the chain. Each participating team has its own board at its disposal. In the board, each team member has its stock and incoming shipments represented by markers, and orders are annotated on a paper, as shown in Fig. 2.

Each player sizes and sends orders to the player who controls the top level, except the factory, which sends orders to its own production line. Each player also receives and must attend orders received from the lower level, except the dealer, who gets their orders from a stack of paper faced down. This stack represents the demand of the final consumer and has the same ordering and values for all

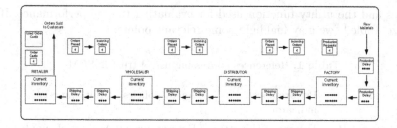

Fig. 2. Board layout for the *Beer Game* [18]

teams. Each player withdraws goods from his stock and sends out shipments to meet the orders of the player controlling the lower level. Each player also receives the shipments shipped from the top level and keeps them in its own stock, except the factory, which receives the shipments from its own production line. If a player does not have sufficient goods in its stock to meet the last order received, the player sends a shipment with the remainder of his stock, and the due portion is noted for shipment in the next round, added to the next order to be satisfied.

The game is divided into a fixed number of rounds, each containing a sequence of actions that must be performed simultaneously by all members of all teams. This sequence is described in Algorithm 1.

Algorithm 1. *Beer Game* - Flow

1: **for all** round **do**
2:    Receive shipment from supplier
3:    Send shipment to client (who will receive it two rounds later)
4:    Record stock on hand or total due
5:    Receive client order
6:    Send order to supplier (who will receive it one round later)
7: **end for**

At the end of the 36th round, the game is closed, and the winning team is determined as being the one that has accumulated, in all its levels and rounds, the lowest score as defined in Eq. (1):

$$score = 0.5 * stock\ on\ hand + 1 * total\ due \tag{1}$$

Consumer demand is revealed: it is fixed at 4 units per round until the 4th round, and then it is changed to 8 rounds from the 5th round until the end of the game.

3   State of the Art

Several works that addressed the use of trust in SCM are listed in Table 1, where we show the performance indicator that determines supplier choices, agents' policies and the utility function used for evaluating the SC performance. If we analyze Table 1, we may highlight some relevant points:

Table 1. References addressing use of trust in SCM

Reference	Performance indicator	Agent policies	Utility function
Akkermans [1]	Volume of shipments received	Heterogeneous	Amount of supplier switches
Schieritz [16]	Volume received and delivery speed	Homogeneous	Amount of supplier switches
Lin, Sung and Lo [12]	Price and delivery time	Homogeneous	Cost, punctuality, cycle time
Kim [10]	Ratio between orders and deliveries	Homogeneous	Stock levels fluctuation
Hou, Xiong, Wang and Liang [9]	Punctual delivery rate	Homogeneous	Working capital and active firms
Giardini, Tosto and Conte [7]	Product quality	Homogeneous	Quality and profit

- In all references, each company of SC corresponds to a simulated agent, but only in [10] agents follow the Beer Game rules;
- In all references, the performance of a supplier is evaluated by the quantity and punctuality of its deliveries;
- Only in [1] heterogeneous decision policies are used in the same simulated SC, with agents that privilege short-term performance of their suppliers, and others that focus on long-term performance;
- Only in [7] agents ask each other for suppliers' suggestions;
- All the papers analyze the impact of agents' actions from the SC's global point of view, but none of them records or compares the profit of each represented company profile.

In our work, we combined some characteristics of these models. Since the Beer Game model is considered a benchmark for this problem, we have also adopted it for our work, like [10]. Like [1], we also enabled heterogeneous decision policies for the agents, since this option is more realistic. Another natural choice is to represent recommendation from peers in our model, like it happens in real cases, as adopted by [7]. Moreover, as we wanted to use a rather simple financial model, we opted to follow the one proposed by [9].

4   Agent-Based SCM Simulation Model

Our research differs from the others by trying to measure the individual performance of agents with different profiles, that may or not use the notion of trust.

These agents interact simultaneously in the same SC modeled according to the rules of *Beer Game*.

In our model, we will refer as i to the agent we are focusing on, as j to its supplier and as K to its set of clients.

4.1 Supply Chain Model

Similarly to [9], the simulated chain is composed of 5 levels: factories, distributors, wholesalers, retailers and final consumers; we considered 20 agents per level. In each round, each agent may order from one supplier at the higher level, as well as fulfill orders made by each of the clients at the lower level.

4.2 Agent Model

In this work, we used an agent architecture composed of:

- **Perception:** the agent detects the shipments sent by its supplier and the orders sent by its customers;
- **Reasoning:** the agent reasons and decides which customers to send the shipments to (first deliver to those who it owes more) and dimension the order to the supplier based on the anchoring and adjustment mechanism described in Sect. 4.3;
- **Action:** the agent sends shipments to his clients and an order to his supplier.

4.3 Ordering by Anchoring and Adjustment Strategy

In [17], the author proposes a model to characterize the way in which companies dimension orders to suppliers in order to control their own stock levels. Such a model is based on the cognitive anchoring and adjustment mechanism (A&A) described in [20], which proposes a heuristic for requests to suppliers so as to:

1. resupply expected inventory losses;
2. reduce the discrepancy between the current and desired stock;
3. maintain a suitable supply line for orders already made but not yet received.

For a more detailed formulation, see [17].

4.4 Working Capital Model

The proposed financial model is based on the one described in [9]. For each agent i, the capital change ΔC_i after each round n is expressed by Eq. (2):

$$\Delta C_i(n) = (\sum_{k \ in \ K} (v_i(n) - p) * O_{ki}(n)) - u * S_i(n) - v_j(n) * O_{ij}(n) \qquad (2)$$

where (i) n is the current round, (ii) $v_i(n)$ is the unit selling price set by i for round n, (iii) p is the unit cost of production, (iv) $O_{ki}(n)$ is the order size made from client k to i in round n, (v) u is the unit storage cost of the stock, (iv) $S_i(n)$ is agent i's stock on hand at the end of round n, (vii) $v_j(n)$ is i's unit buying price from supplier j in round n, and (viii) $O_{ij}(n)$ is the order size made from i to his supplier j in round n.

All these values can vary per round, with the cost prices of each agent corresponding to the sales prices set by its supplier. These prices may vary between v^l_{min} and v^l_{max}, calculated by SC level l, as follows:

1. The cost per unit of stock u per round is agreed to be \$1;
2. The cost of production p is considered the same for each level of the chain, and parameterized in function of u;
3. For the factory, v^0_{min} equals the cost of production p and v^0_{max} equals $v^0_{min} + p$;
4. For each level below, v^l_{min} equals $v^{l-1}_{max} + p$ and v^l_{max} equals $v^l_{min} + p$.

4.5 Supplier Trust Model

To quantify a client i's trust level in a supplier j, we used the approach proposed in [9]. At each round n, the trust level is given by the historical ratio between the shipments delivered in each round and the corresponding orders made three rounds before. Such measure comprises the sum of the transmission delays of the request from the supplier and the sending of the shipments by the latter to its client, as mentioned in the Sect. 2. This ratio is expressed by Eq. (3):

$$Trust_{ij}(n) = \sum_{r=4}^{n} S_{ji}(r) / \sum_{r=1}^{n-3} O_{ij}(r) \qquad (3)$$

where (i) n is the current round, (ii) $O_{ij}(r)$ is the order sent by i to his supplier j in round r, (iii) $S_{ji}(r)$ is the shipment that i received from his supplier j in round r, and (iv) $Trust_{ij}(n)$ is the client i's trust in his supplier j in round n.

4.6 Supplier Recommendation Model

In our model, we consider that an agent may eventually ask his peers for supplier suggestions. With this feature, an agent will possibly have the chance to interact with a better supplier with whom he has never interacted before. We use a parameter ϵ to represent this chance.

4.7 Agent Profiles

Each SC level will consist of agents with different profiles. Each of these profiles will be driven by a goal that incurs a combination of decision policies. Two profiles are proposed in this work:

- **Popular:** A popular agent aims to attract as many clients as possible by offering a low price, and to keep them through the most possible punctual delivery of their orders;

- **Greedy:** A greedy agent aims to maximize its profit by buying cheap, selling expensive and reducing expenses.

We consider that a contract between clients and suppliers holds for d rounds (d is a parameter). After this period, clients reassess trust in their suppliers, eventually asking their peers for new supplier suggestions, and then decide whether to choose a new supplier or keep the current one. This decision process is conditioned to their profile:

- **Popular:** it favors high trust suppliers, since delays in order deliveries lead to a stock shortage for the agent in question, which may render deliveries to its clients unfeasible. To choose a supplier, the agent proceeds as follows:
  1. With ϵ chance, agent selects a random peer among the ones it relies on, and asks him for supplier suggestions;
  2. The chosen peer, if a sincere one, informs all good suppliers it has interacted with so far, with trust rate greater than a threshold 0.5;
  3. The agent then takes the supplier with the highest informed rate and compares with its current supplier. If the first rate is greater than the latter, it switches to the new one;
  4. Otherwise, the agent explores possible better suppliers: it draws a set containing N top-level supplier candidates and chooses among them the one with highest trust. If the chosen supplier has a higher trust level than the current one, the agent switches to the chosen one;
  5. If neither of two steps above occurs, the agents keeps the current supplier.
- **Greedy:** it favors cheaper suppliers. The procedure is analogous to the one followed by popular agents, except that the decision criterion is the cheapest price and the suppliers suggested to them by a peer are the ones that, in the last supply contract with the peer, set a price below half of the interval defined by v_{min} and v_{max} for the supplier's SC level.

In relation to **stock management**, the behaviors of such profiles are:

- **Popular:** it has as desired stock the parameterized safety stock $S*$, in order to prevent against peaks of demand that affect its shipments;
- **Greedy:** it does not maintain a security stock ($S* = 0$), in order to reduce the maintenance cost of its stock.

In order to differentiate **prices** set by each profile, offset δ is provided as parameter, so that:

- **Popular:** it keeps a low price, in order to attract more clients. At each round, it randomly sets the price between v_{min} and $v_{max} - \delta * (v_{max} - v_{min})$, taken from a uniform distribution.
- **Greedy:** it keeps a high price, so as to maximize its profit margin. At each round, it randomly sets the price between $v_{min} + \delta * (v_{max} - v_{min})$ and v_{max}, taken from a uniform distribution.

4.8 Unreliable Peers

At the end of a contract, a client records the price and accumulated trust rate for the contracted supplier in order to suggest it to peers. If, for that same contract, the supplier had been recommended by a peer and it was proven to be a bad one (trust rate lower than 0.5 when asked by popular agent, price in the upper half of the SC level interval when asked by a greedy agent), the peer is marked as unreliable by the client. The peer is not asked for suggestions anymore, and neither answered when he asks for suggestions.

4.9 Liars

In the beginning of each simulation, a fixed share of agents per level on the SC are defined as liars. We represent this fact by a liar rate λ. When asked for suggestions, a liar returns only bad suppliers. To mask its suggestion, the liar transmits each supplier to the peer as if it was a good one, with trust equals (1 − real trust) and price equals ($v_{min} + v_{max}$ − real price).

5 Simulation and Results

5.1 Simulation Cycle

Algorithm 2, used in this work, consists of an extension of Algorithm 1 of the *Beer Game*, described in Sect. 2.

Algorithm 2. Simulation - Flow

 1: Agents initialize inventory, and order and shipment lines
 2: Clients choose one supplier from the top-level members randomly
 3: **for all** round **do**
 4:     Clients receive shipments shipped two rounds earlier by suppliers
 5:     Suppliers pay the cost of production and send shipments to their clients, totally or partially, prioritizing largest due orders
 6:     Suppliers register stock on hand or total due
 7:     Suppliers pay the cost of the stock on hand
 8:     Suppliers receive orders made one round earlier by clients
 9:     **if** end of contract **then**
10:         Suppliers update sales price
11:         Clients review peer trust and supplier trust based on shipments received
12:         Clients decide whether to keep or switch supplier, and which one to switch to
13:     **end if**
14:     Clients size and send request to their suppliers and pay the price set by these
15:     Factory scales and sends production order
16:     Suppliers receive payment for orders placed in the current round by new clients, who buy at the set price
17: **end for**

5.2   Implementation

The project was implemented in ReLogo [15], a domain specific language (DSL) for ABM which incorporates libraries and features of the Repast Simphony framework [2][1].

5.3   Fixed Input Parameters

In our experiments, 50% of agents with Popular profile and 50% with Greedy profile by SC level were combined, in order to determine which strategy prevails over the other if both are adopted by the same number of agents. Another parameter is the demand of the final consumers. For this work, we decided to use random demand: in each round, each final consumer obtains the number of units to be ordered from a uniform distribution, defined in the range of integers between 0 and 12, including the extremes. The other parameters were set empirically, as shown in Table 2.

Table 2. Fixed parameters

Parameter	Description	Value
D	Simulation duration in rounds	200
d	Supply contract duration in rounds - Sect. 4.7	10
L	Agents per SC level	20
S*	Desired (safety) stock - extracted from [17]	48
p	Production cost - Sect. 4.4	10
α_s	Used in stock adjustment - extracted from [17]	0.5
β	α_{sL}/α_s - used in supply line adjustment - extracted from [17]	1.0
Θ	Used in demand forecast - extracted from [17]	0.5
N	Used in supplier choice - Sect. 4.7	5
δ	Differentiates prices between profiles - Sect. 4.7	0.25

5.4   Experiment 1: Impact of Peer Recommendations

In this experiment, all agents were programmed to tell the truth (liar rate $\lambda = 0$), and were subjected to different suggestion rate values (ϵ ranging from 0.0 to 1.0 with 0.1 increment). Each scenario was executed 20 times, and both the mean and standard variation of working capital and trust values at the end of the simulation are shown respectively in Tables 3 and 4.

We can verify that when suggestion rate ϵ increases, working capital tends to increase for popular agents and decrease for greedy ones. A possible reason is that

---

[1] The source available at Github, https://github.com/ajalbut/SupplyChainTrust.

Table 3. Working capital per suggestion rate ϵ

Profile	ϵ	0.0	0.1	0.2	0.3	0.4	0.5	0.6	0.7	0.8	0.9	1.0
Popular	μ	76321	96719	118691	131345	132885	136331	139479	136200	135628	135707	131964
	σ	18002	15202	13511	13039	9007	12359	16474	11269	11986	11599	11414
Greedy	μ	98201	74436	49485	36513	35960	30326	27798	32063	29595	28459	29644
	σ	16861	14563	12716	13218	9160	10977	14044	10327	12047	11035	11637

Table 4. Trust per suggestion rate ϵ

Profile	ϵ	0.0	0.1	0.2	0.3	0.4	0.5	0.6	0.7	0.8	0.9	1.0
Popular	μ	0.792	0.778	0.753	0.741	0.728	0.705	0.710	0.701	0.695	0.662	0.637
	σ	0.017	0.024	0.032	0.031	0.036	0.031	0.046	0.031	0.039	0.036	0.042
Greedy	μ	0.494	0.493	0.471	0.459	0.439	0.409	0.414	0.415	0.383	0.391	0.370
	σ	0.031	0.048	0.040	0.030	0.042	0.041	0.045	0.039	0.029	0.046	0.050

in the long run both popular and greedy agents tend to go for popular suppliers, the first ones aiming for higher trust rates to guarantee their client deliveries and the latter aiming for lower purchase prices to reach higher profit margins. As a consequence, all tend to migrate in the course of simulation. With more sincere recommendations, they gather supplier information faster than exploring on their own, resulting in faster migration and more clients for popular agents.

Moreover, if we analyze some particular cases, when high suggestion rates ϵ effectively generate supplier switching, frequently suppliers do not deliver their goods on time, since it becomes harder for them, whatever their profile is, to predict demand and keep up with orders.

(a) $\epsilon = 0$ (b) $\epsilon = 1$

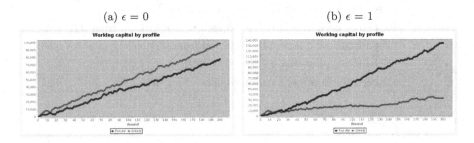

Fig. 3. Difference between low and high suggestion rate ϵ (Color figure online)

Figure 3 illustrates working capital difference between popular and greedy agents in two different individual simulations. When there are no supplier suggestions from peers ($\epsilon = 0$), greedy agents (red line) profit more than popular agents (blue line). On the other hand, when agents always ask for supplier suggestions ($\epsilon = 1$) greedy agents start off better, but are quickly surpassed by popular ones.

5.5 Experiment 2: Impact of Lies

In this experiment, 5 different liar rates were tested (λ ranging from 0.0 to 1.0 with 0.25 increment), combined with 3 different suggestion rates (ϵ equal to 0.25, 0.5 and 0.75), for a total of 15 scenarios. These ϵ values were chosen to represent typical proportional values. Again, each scenario was executed 20 times, and both the mean and standard variation of working capital and trust values at the end of the simulation are shown respectively in Tables 5 and 6.

Regarding the working capital, it is possible to observe that a higher proportion of liars benefits greedy agents and impairs popular ones, since the false

Table 5. Working capital per suggestion rate ϵ and liar rate λ

ϵ	Profile	λ	0.00	0.25	0.50	0.75	1.00
0.25	Popular	μ	118864	116425	109623	91447	85634
		σ	14015	14831	16615	13685	20361
	Greedy	μ	49943	53629	64251	81429	90008
		σ	13659	13286	14932	13699	19394
0.5	Popular	μ	133481	119813	113035	96434	69591
		σ	13406	13987	12019	16804	17042
	Greedy	μ	33453	49698	57569	78974	107241
		σ	11268	13554	11930	16466	15968
0.75	Popular	μ	137345	125819	106664	98942	52685
		σ	12219	12062	17864	13475	14259
	Greedy	μ	28338	43509	64837	75231	123477
		σ	10411	11617	17049	10316	14490

Table 6. Trust per suggestion rate ϵ and liar rate λ

ϵ	Profile	λ	0.00	0.25	0.50	0.75	1.00
0.25	Popular	μ	0.753	0.769	0.785	0.781	0.792
		σ	0.033	0.022	0.025	0.025	0.025
	Greedy	μ	0.459	0.471	0.482	0.505	0.515
		σ	0.039	0.053	0.039	0.035	0.034
0.5	Popular	μ	0.727	0.734	0.770	0.783	0.789
		σ	0.045	0.043	0.032	0.032	0.018
	Greedy	μ	0.433	0.453	0.464	0.498	0.502
		σ	0.038	0.038	0.043	0.038	0.043
0.75	Popular	μ	0.683	0.717	0.737	0.776	0.774
		σ	0.041	0.025	0.039	0.024	0.031
	Greedy	μ	0.414	0.446	0.441	0.468	0.488
		σ	0.026	0.037	0.031	0.046	0.036

recommendations provided by liars tend to point to expensive and unreliable suppliers, which are mostly greedy.

Considering each profile, either popular or greedy, the impact of higher liar rates λ is more significant at higher suggestion rates ϵ, in which case agents adopt suggestions more often and explore less on their own. This may be seen in Fig. 4.

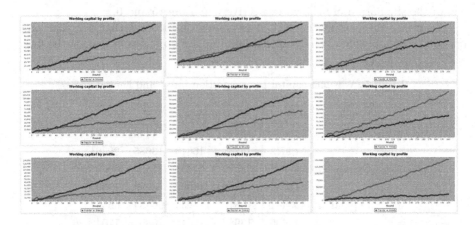

Fig. 4. Working capital evolution for popular (blue) and greedy (red) agents at different liar rates λ (increasing rightward) and suggestion rates ϵ (increasing downward) (Color figure online)

When it comes to trust, popular agents tend to achieve higher levels when there are more liars, and greedy agents when there are less. As it occurred in Experiment 1, it becomes harder for suppliers, whatever their profile is, to predict demand and keep up with orders. Moreover, like the results obtained in Experiment 1, trust level decreases when suggestion rate ϵ increases.

6   Conclusions

In this work, a multi-agent approach was used to simulate a particular SC, namely the *Beer Game*. In the experiments, it was possible to observe the effect of different agent's strategic profiles on their average individual profit. Trust-based client-supplier relationships tend to thrive when there is plenty communication and sincerity, while price-based decisions prevail when silence and/or lies are the norm.

For future experiments, it would be interesting to evaluate the individual benefits of lying compared to telling the truth, as well as to analyse unequal proportions of popular and greedy agents, different supply chain topologies and different values for Beer Game parameters. We could also enable requesting agents to order goods simultaneously from multiple suppliers in a same round. It would be also interesting to test different consumer demand models, instead of just using a random model.

References

1. Akkermans, H.: Emergent supply networks: system dynamics simulation of adaptive supply agents. In: Proceedings of the 34th Annual Hawaii International Conference on System Sciences, p. 11. IEEE Computer Society (2001). https://doi.org/10.1109/HICSS.2001.926299
2. Collier, N.: RePast: an extensible framework for agent simulation. Univ. Chicagos Soc. Sci. Res. **36**, 371–375 (2003). https://doi.org/10.1007/s00114-002-0341-z
3. Croom, S., Romano, P., Giannakis, M.: Supply chain management: an analytical framework for critical literature review. Eur. J. Purch. Supply Manag. **6**(1), 67–83 (2000)
4. De La Fuente, D., Lozano, J.: Application of distributed intelligence to reduce the bullwhip effect. Int. J. Prod. Res. **45**(8), 1815–1833 (2007)
5. Forrester, J.W.: Industrial dynamics. J. Oper. Res. Soc. **48**(10), 1037–1041 (1997)
6. Friedman, M.: The social responsibility of business is to increase its profits. In: Zimmerli, W.C., Holzinger, M., Richter, K. (eds.) Corporate Ethics and Corporate Governance, pp. 173–178. Springer, Heidelberg (2007). https://doi.org/10.1007/978-3-540-70818-6_14
7. Giardini, F., Tosto, G.D., Conte, R.: A model for simulating reputation dynamics in industrial districts. Simul. Model. Pract. Theory **16**(2), 231–241 (2008). https://doi.org/10.1016/j.simpat.2007.11.017
8. Handfield, R.B., Bechtel, C.: The role of trust and relationship structure in improving supply chain responsiveness. Ind. Mark. Manag. **31**(4), 367–382 (2002)
9. Hou, Y., Xiong, Y., Wang, X., Liang, X.: The effects of a trust mechanism on a dynamic supply chain network. Expert Syst. Appl. **41**(6), 3060–3068 (2014). https://doi.org/10.1016/j.eswa.2013.10.037
10. Kim, W.S.: Effects of a trust mechanism on complex adaptive supply networks: an agent-based social simulation study. JASSS **12**(3), 4 (2009)
11. Lambert, D.M., Cooper, M.C.: Issues in supply chain management. Ind. Mark. Manag. **29**(1), 65–83 (2000)
12. Lin, F.R., Sung, Y.W., Lo, Y.P.: Effects of trust mechanisms on supply-chain performance: a multi-agent simulation study. Int. J. Electron. Commer. **9**(4), 9–112 (2005)
13. Mayer, R.C., Davis, J.H., Schoorman, F.D.: An integrative model of organizational trust. Acad. Manag. Rev. **20**(3), 709–734 (1995)
14. Nagurney, A.: Supply Chain Network Economics: Dynamics of Prices, Flows and Profits. Edward Elgar Publishing, Cheltenham (2006)
15. Ozik, J., Collier, N.T., Murphy, J.T., North, M.J.: The ReLogo agent-based modeling language. In: 2013 Winter Simulation Conference (WSC), pp. 1560–1568. IEEE (2013)
16. Schieritz, N.: Emergent structures in supply chains - a study integrating agent-based and system dynamics modeling. In: Proceedings of the 36th Annual Hawaii International Conference on System Sciences, HICSS 2003 (2003). https://doi.org/10.1109/HICSS.2003.1174226
17. Sterman, J.D.: Modeling managerial behavior: misperceptions of feedback in a dynamic decision making experiment. Manag. Sci. **35**(3), 321–339 (1989)
18. Sterman, J.D.: Teaching takes off: flight simulators for management education. OR/MS Today **35**, 40–44 (1992)
19. Swaminathan, J.M., Smith, S.F., Sadeh, N.M.: Modeling supply chain dynamics: a multiagent approach. Decis. Sci. **29**(3), 607–631 (1998). https://doi.org/10.1111/j.1540-5915.1998.tb01356.x

20. Tversky, A., Kahneman, D.: Judgment under uncertainty: heuristics and biases. Science **185**(4157), 1124–1131 (1974). https://doi.org/10.1126/science.185.4157.1124
21. Vlachos, I.P., Bourlakis, M.: Supply chain collaboration between retailers and manufacturers: do they trust each other? Supply Chain Forum: Int. J. **7**, 70–80 (2006)

PASHAMAMA: An Agricultural Process-Driven Agent-Based Model of the Ecuadorian Amazon

Doryan Kaced[1](✉), Romain Mejean[2](✉), Aurélien Richa[3], Benoit Gaudou[1,4,5], and Mehdi Saqalli[2]

[1] UMR 5505 IRIT, CNRS, University Toulouse 1 Capitole, Toulouse, France
doryan.kaced@ut-capitole.fr
[2] UMR 5602 GEODE, CNRS, University Toulouse 2 Jean Jaurès, Toulouse, France
romain.mejean@univ-tlse2.fr
[3] UMR 5505 IRIT, CNRS, University Paul Sabatier, Toulouse, France
[4] Sorbonne University, IRD, UMMISCO, 93143 Bondy, France
[5] USTH - ICTLab, Hanoi, Vietnam

Abstract. This article presents the PASHAMAMA model that aims at studying the situation in the northern part of the Amazonian region of Ecuador in which the intensive oil extraction has induced a high rise of population, pollution, agricultural work and deforestation. It simulates these dynamics impacts on both environment and population by examining exposure and demography over time thanks to a retro-prospective and spatially explicit agent-based approach. Based on a previous work that has introduced roads, immigration and pollution (induced by the oil industry) dynamics, we focus here on the agricultural and the oil salaried work sides of the model. Unlike many models that are highly focused on the use of quantitative data, we choose a process-based approach and rest on qualitative data extracted from interviews with the local population: farmers are not represented by highly cognitive agents, but only attempt to fulfill their local objectives by fulfilling sequentially their constraints (*e.g.* eating before earning money). We also introduce a new evaluation method based on satellite pictures that compares simulated to "real" data on a thematic division of the environment.

Keywords: Agent-based model · Socio-ecological systems · Colonization · Ecuadorian Amazon · Deforestation

1 Introduction

The Northern Ecuadorian Amazon, the region of Ecuador called "Oriente", carries stigmas of a spontaneous agricultural colonization. Encouraged by the State, since the 1970s and 1980s, and then reinforced and facilitated by oil prospecting and exploitation, which opened roads for settlement [3], the region has been the target of a huge migration of inhabitants; this process that can be referred as an agricultural colonization has profoundly altered the landscape.

© Springer Nature Switzerland AG 2019
P. Davidsson and H. Verhagen (Eds.): MABS 2018, LNAI 11463, pp. 59–74, 2019.
https://doi.org/10.1007/978-3-030-22270-3_5

This work takes place in the MONOIL project that aims at developing "a prospective of future dynamics combining contamination exposure, demographics, production activities, with oil but also agriculture, and public policies and their impacts altogether". For this goal, we have developed a spatially explicit agent-based model, named PASHAMAMA [4], integrating the oil leaks and spreading in the environment, and the colonization by families, their settlements and their activities. It is developed on three parishes of the Oriente (Dayuma, Pacayacu and Joya de Los Sachas), but we limit the presentation to Dayuma in this article due to space limitations. This article is focused on the presentation of the socio-economic and demographic part of the model: it aims at tackling the question of the interaction and co-evolution of the colonization and demography with the agri-cultural submodel.

The challenges to develop such a model are multiple and this article provides contributions to face two of them. The first one lies on the shortage of data available on the area and more specifically of data describing human activities: most of the data are available at the global scale. This makes the initialization, dynamics and evaluation on a spatial-explicit model much harder, but it is a common issue to face when building such a large-scale model. The evaluation of such a model in particular is extremely complicated given this lack of data at the proper scale. In particular, among available data, the demography is an input data of the model and can thus not be used to evaluate it. It is possible to get the agricultural production at the scale of Dayuma only, which prevents us to use them to a spatial evaluation. We thus had no choice but to use a proxy to evaluate the spatial accuracy of our model. We thus use land cover maps, based on satellite images classifications and carried out by Ecuadorian government services[1], on which are identified the deforested area. We propose a thematic way to evaluate the model based on a meaningful division of the space.

The second contribution is related to the agent behavior architecture. We argue that, given the lack of data we can gather and in a context of bounded rationality, it is irrelevant to model agent decision-making process with global optimization over all its possible alternatives. On the contrary, we choose an extended KIDS-like [5] approach in which we theorized that agents behavior is highly constraint and they do every task they have to do in the best way they can. They thus perform multiples optimization in a sequential way, which allows to have a good and easy way to implement risk management. The model is thus built from qualitative ground survey results and observations of the people behavioral process. The model had at its core, the process by which the locals make decision about their installation and their land management. This model is process-based, which means that we try to understand and implement the behavior of the locals at the best we can. The behaviour we try to model is the installation of settlers in Dayuma and how they manage their land. We use the pattern of deforestation we get as a proxy value which help us to calibrate and validate the model.

---

[1] *Mapa de cobertura y uso de la tierra del Ecuador continenal año 1990*, Ministerio del Ambiente, 2014.

This paper is organized as follows. Section 2 presents the context of the study and a brief state of the art of related works. Sections 3, 4 and 5 are focused on the model presentation, using the standard O.D.D. protocol [9]. Section 6 shows the preliminary results obtained on the parish of Dayuma in the province of Orellana. Finally Sect. 7 concludes and highlights perspectives.

2 Context

2.1 Historical Context

From the first petrol discovery in 1967, until the beginning of the conflictual and trial era (1990–2000) and the emblematic Aguinda vs. Texaco, Inc. court case in the 1990s [11], our study site (the Northern Ecuadorian Amazon, the region called "Oriente") lived mainly controlled by the Texaco Inc. company that played a central role in local governance, exploiting the petrol resource with a though policy that had a disastrous impact on the environment and human communities.

During this era, the North Oriente was also the object of a colonization plan supported by the various central governments of that time in an effort to relocate the surplus of peasants of the mountain (*Sierra*) and coastal (*Costa*) areas, most of whom lacked land tenure. The plan was supported by two laws (1964 and 1973) that led to the creation of the IERAC (Ecuadorian Institute of Agrarian Reform and Colonization, which organized this colonization) but also to the opening of gravel roads into the forest and connecting oil wells by the petrol company following an agreement with the government. This thus means that the current spatial structure of the colonization reflects the organization of the geological resources more than the potentialities of the surface. Primary forests were therefore exploited for their wood and colonized along and around these roads and tracks: each family of *colonos* received a *finca* (farm) of approximately 50 hectares and had to clear at least half of it for agricultural purposes. The forest lost territory while indigenous communities regressed, either changing their way of life or disappearing. However, progressively effective applications of the law of *comunas* (1937) leased parts of indigenous territories to natives (both locals and those coming from southern provinces, such as some Shuar families), offering some protection thanks to collective land tenure.

Prior to establishing national law to control oil exploitation in 1990, including waste disposal, oil companies did not undertake measures to protect the environment. It is why we stopped our simulation in 1990 with the prospect of adding a political module in the future.

2.2 Related Works

The biophysical processes are based on a previous work presented in [4] which focus on oil hazards in the area and their impact on inhabitants. It has been developed using the generic agent-based modeling and simulation GAMA platform [8]. This first model lacked farmers' agricultural behavior model to manage their exploitation and make their decision in terms of cropping.

The use of Agent-Based Models (ABMs) to study Socio-environmental Systems has now widely spread in the modeling community [17] and the description of agents representing human beings (*e.g.* farmers) with decision to make is still a really challenging task. According to [1], many approaches, derived from economic and social sciences theories, have been used to model farmers' behaviour in relation with natural systems in ABMs. Firstly, the micro-economic approach, which consists of agents maximizing an utility function based on revenue or profit, rely on the assumption of rational agents (homo economicus) (*e.g.* [16] among many others). Then and more, a psychological and cognitive approach integrating more abilities for agents and their aspirations, beliefs and intentions as well as social structures effects like social norms or social reproduction. In this way, [6] used a specific framework for their agents, that integrate behavioural drivers, in their study of the use of pesticides in Colombia. Similarly, [7] used Belief Function Theory to model yearly decision-making process of cropping plan in the South-East of France. Other models, from a participatory approach, directly involve stakeholders in the modelling process [18]. Also, KIDS models are driven by empirical data [10]: [15] have developed an ABM on the Ecuadorian Amazon used to simulate land use change on farms, based on empirical rules from a socio-economic and demographic survey; [2] have used a cluster analysis on empirical data to distinguish four types of farmers' agents in a spatially explicit model based on cadastral information. Recently, [12] reviewed ABMs for agricultural policy evaluation.

The next three sections are dedicated to the model description using the O.D.D. protocol (Overview, Design Concepts, Details) [9].

3 Overview

3.1 Purpose

The aim of the model is to reproduce the evolution of the parish (*parroquia*) of Dayuma under the impact of the migration of Escuadorian farmers in the Amazonian forest induced by the petrol exploitation of the area and their settlement.

We aims at reproducing the migration and settlement of Ecuadorian farmers in the Amazonian forest induced by the petrol exploitation of the area and at observing its consequences in terms of deforestation (for agricultural purpose).

3.2 Entities, State Variables, and Scales

Scales. As detailed in the input data presented in the Sect. 5.2, the modeled system is an area of approximately 87 km by 58 km. In this area, we chose as smallest spatial unit, the plot, that is the agricultural unit in our model. A plot is defined as a square with an edge of 90 m (for the high resolution Digital Elevation Model).

The simulations are launched from the 1st of January 1960 and run until the 31st of December 1990, with a simulation step lasting 1 month.

Entities. As presented previously, our main interest is to study the colonization and the anthropization of the parish of Dayuma over a long period of time (30 years). This process should take into account arrivals of new settlers and their allocation of a new `finca` (driven by the evolution of the `road` network), but also the development of the agricultural activity and its effect on the landscape. We thus made the hypothesis that the `family` is the key entity in this process (rather than the individual). We have introduced individual `person` and `couple` to simulate the demography, *i.e.* aging, wedding and new individual birth processes. The evolution of the number of inhabitants has an influence on the food needs and working force of each family and thus on the agricultural process, and finally the territory land cover. Agriculture relies on two kinds of entities: human activities and decision-making and physical support. The family think its agriculture activities at the scale of the `finca` with individual implementations at `plot` scale. We made the choice for modularity purpose to introduce the `finca_manager` agent that manages the `activity` set for the whole *finca* and in particular their `activity_state` that evolve step by step. We also made the choice to split the set of activities (coffee, market gardening...) into `subsistence_activity`, necessary to feed the family, and `payout_activity`, that provides financial incomes.

To make its decision about new activities, the `family` via the `finca_manager` needs to know the history of its own production, the `market` price and via the `path_manager` the price and time to send it to the market.

These entities, their main attributes and relations are summarized in the class diagram presented in Fig. 1. Only the main attributes and operations are presented in the diagram (in particular attributes used only for internal computations are not displayed).

Environment Variables. The environment variables are mostly used to initialize the family state: initial capital (in dollars), the number of working day per month and of working hour per day. We also have the price of every production and the demography (number of inhabitants, birth rate ...) at each time step.

We initialized the capital of each family at 150 dollars to explicit that they don't have many resources. We have put as a hypothesis the amount of work that a human can do in a month. We attribute to every adult 20.5 Human Day per month and to every child or elderly half this amount. During every day, a human can work 8 h. We also have the price of every production at each time step, the demography, the legal context in order to be able to change them in futures studies and use them to test the effect of different politics.

3.3 Process Overview and Scheduling

At each simulation step, the processes are scheduled sequentially in order to avoid unexpected side effects of possible interactions. First the demography is applied: it updates the family population and installs the new people on *fincas*. Then the bio-physical environment is updated: the biomass of each plot, the roads and markets are updated given preloaded data. The path manager gives for every plot, the time and the price for every activity to go from one plot to the

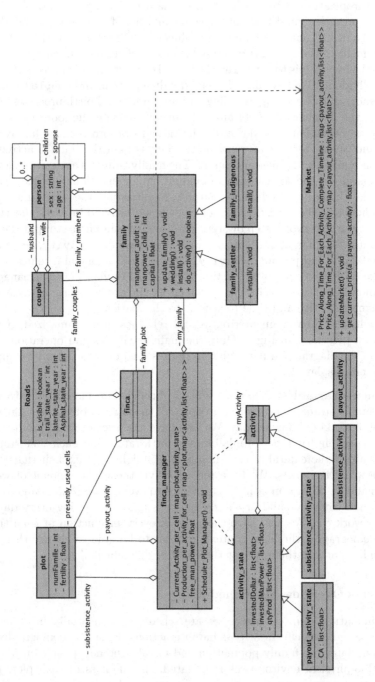

Fig. 1. UML class diagram

market of the map. Finally, families can start managing their *finca, i.e.* exploiting it with the constraints of first trying to feed the family members and only in case of remaining working time, earn money.

4   Design Concepts

As recommended by the authors of the O.D.D. protocol [9], only the relevant Design Concepts are presented below.

Objectives. The main objectives of the families are first to produce enough for their needs (through subsistence crops) and then to maximize their incomes with wage-earning and crash crops taking into account their current amount of money and their available working force. The self-feeding is divided in two objectives. The first one is the need to produce enough proteins for the entire family and the second one is to produce enough calories for everyone in the family. Families will produce enough proteins and its associated calories and will try to reach the total amount of needed calories through carbohydrates (carbohydrate here).

We do not take into account vitamins because the gardening tends to produce enough of it.

Learning. We make the hypothesis that families have a poor knowledge on their ground fertility but a good knowledge on their past productions depending on the activity and the plot. Each family will thus remember its production plot each crop was made on, to better know their ground and thus better predict their future incomes.

This limited knowledge prevent them to predict their future generated incomes by each crop. But over the simulation they will observe this production and learn to have a better knowledge over their ground. The learning revolve around a perfect memory for previous events. No fog of war is used. Every family will remember its production and the fertility of the plot each crop was made on.

Interaction. In addition to the use of learning, families try to improve their knowledge by asking neighbor families an estimation of their production if they don't already have their own information. Families choose to only take into account the information given by the family which is in the closest situation about to the use of one type of production on one plot.

Families can share information. When a family has no knowledge on the production it can expect, it will ask an estimation to the neighbouring family. Each family with knowledge on this matter will then provide information about their productions. The asking family will only take the information given by the knowing neighbour which had this activity on a plot with the closest estimated fertility to the one family want to use.

Sensing. To make their decisions, families have different information coming from their sensing: they have a perfect perception of the price markets and their ground fertility. Families have knowledge over the state of the transport network: they have access to the time and price, and manpower needed to send their productions from their farm to the marker.

Adaptation. The simulations are run over 30 years with a step of 1 month; during this period of time, both the bio-physical (route network or soil fertility) and socio-economic (activity prices or demography) environments evolve. The families have to adapt to theses changes by abandoning less-profitable activities to settle new ones that can bring more incomes.

Prediction. At several steps in the family behavior, it needs to make some choice depending on the production an activity can give on a plot. It can be the case to predict whether the family is self-sufficient (*i.e.* it produces enough food to feed all the family[2]) or to choose which activity is the best to install on a given plot (in particular because both the turnover and the expenses are computed from the production). In order to predict the production of a plot for a given activity, the family extracts from its knowledge all the time it had a production of this activity. It then looks at the production made by the plot with the closest fertility and use it as the predicted value and thus an estimator of the production on the given plot.

At different moment, the family have to make choice depending on the production an activity can give on a plot. In order to succeed in this task, it will extract from its knowledge all the time it produce crops of this activity and the fertility of the relief it was made on. It will then look at the production made by the plot with the closest fertility and use it as a predicted value.

The family have to predict if it will be self-sufficient (if it will produce enough food to feed all the family). In order to succeed in this task, it must know of all the macronutrients it needs and an estimation of the macronutrients produced by the subsistence crops. The needed macronutrients are calculated according to [13]. The produced macronutrients are calculated by predicting the total amount of each crop we produced and summing the associated macronutrients. If all the predicted produced macronutrients are superior or equal to the needed macronutrients, the family is self-sufficient.

The family needs to predict the gross incomes gained by putting an activity on a plot, in order to choose which activity is the best. In order to do this, the family will have to predict the turnover and the expenses. Both needs to predict the production. The turnover is calculated by multiplying the price per kilogram of a crop by the number of crops in kilograms produced. The expenses are a sum of the taxes on the turnover and the cost of sending the production to the market.

Stochasticity. The main stochastic part of the model is the evolution of the population: in particular, the initial number of individuals in each settler family is random. We use the demographic data to get the new number of people that will get in Dayuma, but the existing families update themselves randomly given the birth and mortality rate. Then we create a number of families which is equal to the number of new people coming divided by the average number of people in

---

[2] The macronutrients are calculated given an activity production based on [13].

a family. In the family, the number of children is between 2 and 5, the number of adult between 2 and 4 and the number of old people between 0 and 2. The chief is the oldest person in the family.

There is also an element of stochasticity on the production of every activity. The maximal production has a top and bottom bound and the actual production is calculated according to the quality of the plot and the calculated maximal production. The work in the oil industry is stochastic too: family members only have a certain chance of getting a one-month job, at each time step. The salary is set between 300 and 400 dollars per month.

Collectives. The model contains two main collectives: the family and the *finca*. The family is the entity that takes all the decisions in terms of agriculture development, *i.e. finca* management (through the proxy entity finca_manager). It is composed of individuals and couples: these two kinds of entities are integrated in the model only to manage the demography part of the model. They are also used to compute the family working force and its food need. The *finca* is only the administrative property of the family and gather all the plots it contains, but all the dynamics are implemented at the plot scale.

Observation. During the simulation, we observe activities productions and the money amount of families. We also observe the final map of forest/deforestation (produced in the model given the plot biomass) with the intention to compare it with actual satellite image, in order to evaluate our model. This final indicator is the one that is used to compare the results of the simulation to the real deforestation rate.

5 Details

5.1 Initialization

- We initialize the plots from the Digital Elevation Model of Dayuma. Every plot has an initial surface, fertility and biomass. Its biomass is calculated according to the local biomass.
- The position of the market is initialized at the place that is extracted from the real-life data. And the *fincas* and *communas* are created from input data.
- For the entire duration of the simulation, the same set of activity is used. We have 7 of them, 3 being annuity farming (coffee, cacao and breeding) and 4 subsistence farming (plantain banana, market gardening, corn/manioc and small breeding).
- We initialize the family capital to 150 dollars, the working time of an adult to 20.5 Human days per month and half of it for a child or an elderly and a day to 8 h.

5.2 Input Data

First, the input data contain multiple spatial data: the shapefile of Dayuma bounds, the shapefile of main roads (with, for each road, its construction date, its state (trail, laterite or asphalt) and its mean transport speed), a shapefile of pedology (containing in particular fertility data), a cadastre file (a shapefile or the *fincas* and *communas*) and the Digital Elevation Model of the area (with a resolution of $90\,\mathrm{m} \times 90\,\mathrm{m}$).

In addition, the input data includes a tabular file with the demography for every month after 1960: it contains the total population, its evolution, the birthrate and the migration. Finally, the simulation needs a file that contains every subsistence or crop activity. For each activity, we can extract every data we need to do those activities, including the transport cost: the cost in man power or money for installation and maintenance, the maximum or minimum production, the lowest fertility on which we can produce crops with this activity, the questioning frequency, the necessary surface to do it and the max number of plots we can put this activity on. For the subsistence activities, we have the percentage of carbohydrates or proteins contained in the production. Finally, we have a file that provides selling prices for each cash crop and for every year.

5.3   Submodels

The Colonization Submodel. At every time step, this model will simulate the demography of Dayuma. Families will be created and install themselves. 51% of the created families are settlers and the 49% remaining ones are indigenous. The indigenouses install themselves in the *communa*, with other indigenous families and are assigned a farm on which they have the operating rights. The settlers install themselves near the roads and in the *finca* that is the closest to the market.

The main stochastic part of the model is the evolution of the population: in particular, the initial number of individuals in each settler family is chosen randomly. We use the demographic data to get the new number of people that will get in Dayuma. We make the existing family update themselves with the birth and mortality rate. Then we create a number of families which is equal to the number of new people coming divided by the average number of people in a family. In the family, the number of children is between 2 and 5, the number of adult between 2 and 4 and the number of old people between 0 and 2. The chief is the oldest person in the family.

The Market Submodel. The market find for every cash crop the price at which it is sold for the current year in the simulation and gives it to the family.

The Farming Submodel. The family has two objectives (in the following priority order): to produce enough food to feed all the family members and maximizing its money incomes. At every step, the family behavior can be described by the following steps:

1. **Prepare each plot for its activity.** In order to install an activity on a plot or to maintain already installed activities, the plot must have enough free space. The family ensures that this is the case for every active plot, otherwise it prepares it (*i.e.* and thus destroy the exceeding biomass). Preparation has

a cost, both in time and money, that is conditioned by the activity. This cost will be in money and in man power because it takes time and the family might have to rent a chainsaw and gasoline to cut the excess in biomass. This action is made for every plot, even the plot that are producing, because the family must maintain its crops.

2. **Do subsistence farming.** The subsistence farming has a cost in man power and it is done before the cash crops because it is more important to feed the family than to get money. From this activity, family members will get the needed proteins and carbohydrates.

3. **Work for the oil industry.** This activity costs 20.5 Human Day per month and earns money in order to create exploitations. The chance of getting a job follows a linear function which is at 10% in 1960 and 1% in 1990. They do this work before the cash crops only if they have less than 1,000 dollars in capital. If not, they prefer to add new cash crop activities and postpone trying to work in industry to the end of the step, if remaining working time is available.

4. **Do cash crops.** At this step, the family will do its activity of cash crops in order to get money. It is at this step that it will produce, send and sell its production.

5. **Question the activities and remove the useless ones if necessary.** At every step, the family checks if its active plots still have enough fertility. Furthermore, every activity must be questioned at some interval. Cash and subsistence activities are not questioned with the same criteria. In order to know if a subsistence activity must be stopped, the family checks if it produces too much food (30% more here) and if it is the case, it drops one activity while maximizing the food diversity. In the case of crops activity, it will check if it produces enough food and if it does not, it might have to delete the less profitable crop activity in order to free some manpower.

6. **Put in fallow the plots with less than 30% of fertility.**

7. **Add a new activity on a plot if possible.** The choosing of the plot on which the activity is done with the following Criterion of Selection.

$$CS(x,t) = \frac{p(t) + Fertility(x,t)}{(D(x) + 1).(l(x) + 1)}$$

with $D(x)$ the distance to the closest exiting plot of the *paroquia* of the plot x; $p(t)$: a random number in order to shuffle the plot with the closest score; $l(x)$ the risk of flood on the plot x. At this point, we have the choice between adding a cash crops activity or a subsistence farming activity. First, the family tries to predict if it is self-sufficient in food. If it is not, it adds a subsistence activity. If it is, it adds a cash activity. The adding of a subsistence activity is done according to the principle of plurality of the crops. Every family will try to diversify its food intake. So the family will try to have the same number of plot on each subsistence activity. When multiple activities don't have the same amount of occurrences as the most done activity of subsistence, we rank them accordingly to the inverse of the manpower needed to do the activity and install the best. If we want to add a cash crop, the family will estimate for every possible activity the gross income it could generate. The best activity will be installed on the plot. This process is explained in the prediction part of the design concept.

6   First Results

Due to lack of precise data, we cannot evaluate the simulation outputs directly with the real corresponding data, such as the spatial distribution of crops. As a proxy, we use the deforestation as the only indicator we can evaluate. As reference data, we choose to use a map extracted from satellite data by identifying deforested plots. In order to evaluate our model, we thus compare the level of deforestation in our simulation outputs[3] and the one recorded in the region of Dayuma in 1990, extracted from land use and land cover maps[4].

Due to our lack of data, we opted for a grid-based method to evaluate the outputs, rather than pixel to pixel methods (statistical indices like Cohen's kappa or confusion matrices), because we had no interest in reproducing pixel-precise dynamics for a process-based model. The pixel-to-pixel evaluation method consists in computing the number of pairs of pixels from the real data and simulated data that are different[5]. This distance is thus not that interesting because we want to know where the settlers came; and how they impacted the field is just a consequence of his/her behavior. From our point of view, there is no difference between using one plot or the one that is just next to it because it is still in his farm. We want to see if our agents have proportionally the same amount of effect on their land than the settler who was in the same situation.

Therefore, in order to compute the grid-based error indicator, we created a grid with a mesh of five squared kilometres covering the entirety of our study area, for which we calculated a proportion of deforested pixels (on the one hand from satellite image classification data and on the other hand from simulation data) by mesh in a geographic information system (GIS). Then, the layers are subtracted from each other (deforestation rate in simulation data - deforestation rate in satellite image classification data), to obtain a deviations map (Fig. 2) which indicates over-estimations and under-estimations of deforestation by the model. We can see on it that the model over-estimates forest clearing for the most part, especially in the northern and in the southern parts of the study area (up to 24.4% of over-estimation in some meshes). However, there is a bias related to the presence of a side effect, which we have tried to limit (without losing too much information) by eliminating from the analysis the border meshes of which less than half of the pixels were included in the study area. This evaluation method just give us an evaluation at a larger scale than the pixel-to-pixel method but doesn't allow us to test our assumptions. Here our assumption are that settler

---

[3] Deforested pixels are plots where at least 50% of the biomass is missing.

[4] We consider as "deforested" pixels belonging to the categories "populated areas" and "agricultural land" of level 1 of *Mapa de cobertura y uso de la tierra del Ecuador continenal año 1990*, Ministerio del Ambiente (MAE), 2014.

[5] It is thus close to the classical Hamming distance [14].

want to be able to travel as fast as possible to the city, so they choose well-connected farms and the oil industry has an impact on the amount of money that the farmers have and thus on the amount of work they can do, which has a big impact of the land. Moreover, farmers in well-connected roads have to pay less to make theirs products travel to the market and have more money at the end of the month to invest in their farm.

A similar but more thematic and spatial approach to evaluate the simulation outputs of the model was used using the road network (Fig. 3). Indeed, given the role of the road network in the colonization process, it seemed interesting to take it as a reference point for the evaluation of simulation data. Thus, four zones, corresponding to different buffers around the roads (from one kilometre to ten kilometres and more), were used to calculate the same deforestation rates as previously. This thematic method allows us to spatially evaluate our results: over-estimations appear lower (less than 3% from one to five kilometres around roads) and underestimations are negligible (less than 1% beyond ten kilometres around roads).

We propose a global method of evaluating spatial results according to buffers that are made to test initial assumptions. It allows us to test the model and check if our assumptions can generate the expected results. Two type of error can be seen here:

– First there are error of modeling because we can see that in places that are not at all well-connected, there are still a few places that are deforested, and thus there are people who came here. We cannot explain why. Our assumptions still are coherent with the majority of the settlers, but are not complete.
– Second, there might be fine-tuning errors (or still modeling errors) because we are overestimating deforestation in well-connected areas.

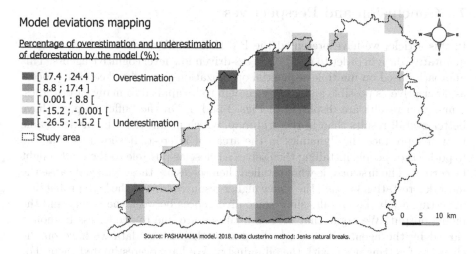

Fig. 2. Deforestation error by grid (in 1990)

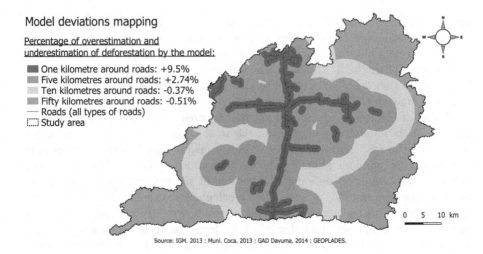

Fig. 3. Deforestation error by buffer (in 1990)

The separation of space according to our assumptions allows us to see easily what went wrong with the modeling process and how we can improve our model, either by fine-tuning the parameters or changing our assumptions. Here, we see that most errors are concentrated on the zone around one kilometer from the roads. It could mean that our understanding of the phenomenon in this area in particular is not that good. It allows us to confront our expectation of the spatial organization for the studied phenomenon and can help us understand the localized effect of our assumptions and thus what we must change.

7   Conclusion and Perspectives

In this article, we have presented the PASHAMAMA model and how we used qualitative data in order to design process-driven low-level cognitive agents. This approach based on multiple sequential optimizations is used to keep the process as descriptive as possible and generic enough to be applied to many case studies. Simulation results are displayed in Figs. 2 and 3. On the buffer map, we have better overall results than in the grid map, which means that the model is able to well reproduce the dynamics in the areas of interest. It shows us that the hypothesis of people installing themselves as close as possible to the roads might be correct. The first people who installed themselves are those who will cause the most deforestation because they have higher resources due to the high probability of getting a job. The results show some divergences between the reality and the model output. We argue that over-estimations are due to the excess in money earned by the agents: it seems to be due to the lack of data we have on the chances of getting a job with the oil industry. We have overestimated them. For the under-estimation, they are two kind. First, we cannot explain why people settle near isolated areas. The second kind is about the places with high under-estimation (near 25%) where there are settlers, but they can not earn enough money to have an efficient enough farm (and thus deforest).

Here, we can see that our model over-estimate the impact and efficiency of the first settlers that are close to the roads and might under-estimate that of the newcomers.

The work presented here is only a first step. In particular, the agricultural module still needs tuning on some parameters: after preliminary studies, the most important of them is the probability of getting a work in the oil industry. We need to design a function computing the hiring rate given the oil production and the cost of the oil barrel. This model needs to be extended to help us to understand more dynamics in Dayuma. We will consider the addition of a policy module in which the institutions will be able to put some rules for the agricultural production, oil production, or for the installation of health institutions.

Acknowledgment. This study was partly funded by the French research funding agency ANR (Agence Nationale de la Recherche), two French research institutions, the "Institut des Amériques" and "Maison des Sciences de l'Homme et de la Société de Toulouse" (USR CNRS 3414), ECOLAB Funds, Occitanie region and university of Toulouse. The team received logistical support from the IRD.

References

1. An, L.: Modeling human decisions in coupled human and natural systems: review of agent-based models. Ecol. Model. **229**, 25–36 (2012)
2. Bakker, M.M., van Doorn, A.M.: Farmer-specific relationships between land use change and landscape factors: introducing agents in empirical land use modelling. Land Use Policy **26**(3), 809–817 (2009)
3. Bilsborrow, R.E., Barbieri, A.F., Pan, W.: Changes in population and land use over time in the Ecuadorian Amazon. Acta Amaz. **34**(4), 635–647 (2004)
4. Chapotat, W., et al.: An agent-based model of the Amazonian forest colonisation and oil exploitation: the Oriente study case. In: Sauvage, S., Sanchez Perez, J.-M., Rizzoli, A.E. (eds.) iEMSs, vol. 5, pp. 1335. iEMSs (2016)
5. Edmonds, B., Moss, S.: From KISS to KIDS – an 'anti-simplistic' modelling app-roach. In: Davidsson, P., Logan, B., Takadama, K. (eds.) MABS 2004. LNCS (LNAI), vol. 3415, pp. 130–144. Springer, Heidelberg (2005). https://doi.org/10.1007/978-3-540-32243-6_11
6. Feola, G., Binder, C.R.: Towards an improved understanding of farmers' behaviour: the integrative agent-centred (IAC) framework. Ecol. Econ. **69**(12), 2323–2333 (2010)
7. Gaudou, B., et al.: The MAELIA multi-agent platform for integrated analysis of interactions between agricultural land-use and low-water management strategies. In: Alam, S.J., Parunak, H.V.D. (eds.) MABS 2013. LNCS (LNAI), vol. 8235, pp. 85–100. Springer, Heidelberg (2014). https://doi.org/10.1007/978-3-642-54783-6_6
8. Grignard, A., Taillandier, P., Gaudou, B., Vo, D.A., Huynh, N.Q., Drogoul, A.: GAMA 1.6: advancing the art of complex agent-based modeling and simulation. In: Boella, G., Elkind, E., Savarimuthu, B.T.R., Dignum, F., Purvis, M.K. (eds.) PRIMA 2013. LNCS (LNAI), vol. 8291, pp. 117–131. Springer, Heidelberg (2013). https://doi.org/10.1007/978-3-642-44927-7_9

9. Grimm, V., Berger, U., DeAngelis, D.L., Polhill, J.G., Giske, J., Railsback, S.F.: The ODD protocol: a review and first update. Ecol. Model. **221**, 2760–2768 (2010)
10. Janssen, M.A., Ostrom, E.: Empirically based, agent-based models. Ecol. Soc. **12**(2) (2006)
11. Juteau-Martineau, G., Becerra, S., Maurice, L.: Ambiente, petróleo y vulnerabilidad política en el oriente ecuatoriano: ¿hacia nuevas formas de gobernanza energética? América Lat. Hoy **67**, 119–137 (2014)
12. Kremmydas, D., Athanasiadis, I.N., Rozakis, S.: A review of agent based modeling for agricultural policy evaluation. Agric. Syst. **164**, 95–106 (2018)
13. Laure, J.: Nutrition et population en vue de la planification alimentaire. ORSTOM, PARIS (1983)
14. MacWilliams, F.J., Sloane, N.J.A.: The Theory of Error-Correcting Codes. Elsevier, Amsterdam (1977)
15. Mena, C.F., Walsh, S.J., Frizzelle, B.G., Xiaozheng, Y., Malanson, G.P.: Land use change on household farms in the Ecuadorian Amazon: design and implementation of an agent-based model. Appl. Geogr. **31**(1), 210–222 (2011)
16. Saqalli, M., Bielders, C.L., Gerard, B., Defourny, P.: Simulating rural environmentally and socio-economically constrained multi-activity and multi-decision societies in a low-data context: a challenge through empirical agent-based modeling. J. Artif. Soc. Soc. Simul. **13**(2), 1 (2010)
17. Schulze, J., Müller, B., Groeneveld, J., Grimm, V.: Agent-based modelling of social-ecological systems: achievements, challenges, and a way forward. J. Artif. Soc. Soc. Simul. **20**(2) (2017)
18. Voinov, A., Bousquet, F.: Modelling with stakeholders. Environ. Model. Softw. **25**(11), 1268–1281 (2010)

The MASON Simulation Toolkit: Past, Present, and Future

Sean Luke[1]([✉]), Robert Simon[1], Andrew Crooks[1], Haoliang Wang[1], Ermo Wei[1], David Freelan[1], Carmine Spagnuolo[2], Vittorio Scarano[2], Gennaro Cordasco[3], and Claudio Cioffi-Revilla[1]

[1] George Mason University, Washington, DC, USA
{sean,simon}@cs.gmu.edu
{acrooks2,hwang17,ewei,dfreelan,ccioffi}@gmu.edu
[2] Università degli Studi di Salerno, Salerno, Italy
cspagnuolo@unisa.it, vitsca@dia.unisa.it
[3] Università degli Studi della Campania "Luigi Vanvitelli", Naples, Italy
gennaro.cordasco@unicampania.it

Abstract. MASON is a widely-used open-source agent-based simulation toolkit that has been in constant development since 2002. MASON's architecture was cutting-edge for its time, but advances in computer technology now offer new opportunities for the ABM community to scale models and apply new modeling techniques. We are extending MASON to provide these opportunities in response to community feedback. In this paper we discuss MASON, its history and design, and how we plan to improve and extend it over the next several years. Based on user feedback will add distributed simulation, distributed GIS, optimization and sensitivity analysis tools, external language and development environment support, statistics facilities, collaborative archives, and educational tools.

Keywords: Agent-based simulation · Open source · Library

1 Introduction

MASON is an open source single-process simulation core and visualization toolkit in Java, designed to be used for a wide range of models, but with a special emphasis on agent-based models involving up to millions of agents. MASON has support for geographical information systems (GIS) and social networks, among other areas. Agent-based models (or ABMs) have taken hold not just in the sciences [10,17,18], but also in engineering areas such as distributed systems, swarm robotics, multiagent learning, and artificial life: for example, swarms of drones, driverless cars, air traffic control, and factory floor robots [11,16,19]. MASON was designed to serve both of these worlds.

Swarm-style multiagent simulation toolkits have developed along two lines. The first line to emerge were libraries geared for easy development of simple models. These toolkits usually were single-threaded, generally tied the model to

© Springer Nature Switzerland AG 2019
P. Davidsson and H. Verhagen (Eds.): MABS 2018, LNAI 11463, pp. 75–86, 2019.
https://doi.org/10.1007/978-3-030-22270-3_6

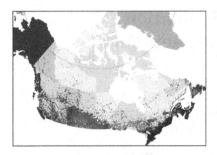

Fig. 1. Model of impact of climate change on Canadian communities [14].

Fig. 2. MASON running on-board collaborative real time soccer robots [22].

its visualization and other facilities, and often deemphasized efficiency. Examples include SWARM [9], NetLogo [5], and perhaps early versions of Repast [7].

The second line consisted of tools meant for large, complex simulations that might be run many times. These toolkits emphasized efficiency and extensibility more heavily, but were still generally single-process. MASON was among the first toolkits in this second line, and introduced many (for ABMs) unique features, including multithreaded models, separation of model and visualization, fully self-contained models, model serialization and migration, 3D visualization, and an orthogonal, consistent, and small design emphasizing efficiency. Other toolkits (for example Repast) have also advanced in many of these areas since then.

As computational cost decreases and models become more complex, we think that a new trend is emerging in ABM models: a third generation of simulation tools which give multiagent systems researchers access to high performance distributed simulation and the capabilities made possible by it: such as distributed GIS models and automated model validation and optimization. Some high-profile tools have made strides in some of these directions (such as FLAME [4] and Repast HPC [8], among others). At the same time, these third-generation toolkits must be clean, easily customized, and provide significant coding support. It would be desirable, though challenging, to marry these features with the traditional ease of use and accessibility afforded by some earlier systems.

Following the recommendations of a 2013 MASON community workshop [20], we are extending MASON to a full-featured third-generation toolkit. In this paper we discuss MASON's history, its architecture, where we think it needs improvement, and our plans for enhancing MASON over the next few years.

2   Development History

Though it has found use in the social science and computational biology ABM fields, MASON was originally meant for multirobotics and multiagent learning, and to evaluate evolved swarm behaviors produced by the ECJ evolutionary computation toolkit [3]. However after discussion with the GMU Center for Social Complexity, MASON's team realized that the modeling overlap between swarm

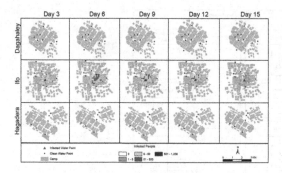

Fig. 3. Modeling the spread of cholera in the Dadaab refugee camp complex in Kenya [15].

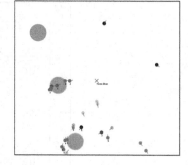

Fig. 4. Box-pulling model with 625 swarm robots [21].

robotics, AI, and ABMs in the social sciences was unusually high, and so decided to create a general-purpose library to serve the ABM community writ large.

MASON had several design goals from the very beginning. *First,* MASON was designed to have a small, high-performance, self-contained simulation core so that many models could be run in parallel, or could involve up to millions of agents. *Second,* MASON was designed to produce guaranteed identical results regardless of architecture when possible. *Third,* MASON was created with a Model-View-Controller (MVC) architecture with complete separation between the model and the visualization, and with model serialization. *Fourth,* as it came from the robotics community, MASON was meant to support a wide range of visualization facilities, including both 2D and 3D support. *Fifth,* MASON was designed to be very easily modified and extended.

These goals are hardly unusual in the general simulation community. However to our knowledge, among the major ABM toolkits at the time (such as SWARM, Repast, NetLogo and Ascape [1]) MASON's combination of design goals was original. MASON was released at Agent 2003, and we think it has had a significant impact on both the design and implementation of ABM tools since then.

Because of its emphasis on customization, efficiency, and generality, MASON has been used in a wide range of models, from small to very large, and in fields from robotics to the social sciences. As illustration, Figs. 1, 2, 3 and 4 show four uses drawn from our own experience. For example, we have used MASON to build a 10-million agent model of permafrost thawing and its consequences on Canadian communities [14] (Fig. 1); and we have also used MASON running on-board cooperative soccer-playing robots during RoboCup [22] (Fig. 2).

3   MASON's Design

As a roughly MVC architecture, MASON is broken into two pieces, as shown in Fig. 5. The first part is the *model* (the simulation proper) and the second part is the *visualization.* Unless one chooses to have model objects display themselves,

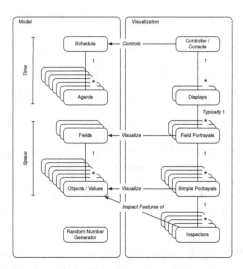

Fig. 5. Illustration of MASON's top-level architecture

the model and visualization are entirely separated, enabling model serialization and the removal or reinstatement of the visualization mid-run.

Model and Visualization. A MASON simulation is encapsulated in a top-level model object which contains a simple real-valued time *schedule* on which are registered one or more *agents* to be called at some time in the future. Additionally, the model may hold one or more *fields* to represent space. MASON provides many fields, such as square or hex grids of objects or values, continuous space, and graphs or multigraphs. Many fields can be 2D or 3D; bounded, toroidal, or unbounded; and sparse or dense; and you can create your own as you see fit. Last but not least, MASON provides utilities for multithreading and a high-quality random number generator. Models can be fully serializable, self-contained, and capable of running side-by-side in multiple threads or in the same thread.

MASON provides 2D and 3D visualization tools, plus plug-in visualization facilities such as for GIS. Model visualization is encapsulated in a special top-level object. This contains a *controller* whose job is to start, stop, and otherwise manipulate the schedule. The most common controller is a window called a *console*. The controller also manages some number of windows called *displays* that handle 2D or 3D visualization. A display helps the user manipulate and visualize various fields by stacking together one or more *field portrayals*. A field portrayal often portrays individual objects or values in fields by calling forth a custom *simple portrayal* designed to visualize that particular object or value. Objects may choose to portray themselves as well. If the user selects portrayed objects with the mouse, a simple portrayal may create *inspectors* to provide object details, trace the objects through charts and graphs, and so on.

Utilities and Extensions. MASON has many utilities to support model design. These include random number distributions, Java Bean Properties inspectors, GUI widgets, movie and picture generation, and chart creation. Several of MASON's utility objects have since found their way into other ABM toolkits (like NetLogo).

Finally, MASON is often extended to serve special functions. Foremost is *GeoMASON*, which adds high-quality GIS capabilities to MASON, including first-in-class raster and vector data model integration, standardized data and file formats, query algorithms, visualization, and integration with external GIS tools. GeoMASON sits atop the Java Topology Suite (JTS).

MASON is also integrated with ECJ [3], a popular, massively distributed evolutionary computation toolkit with which MASON was intended to dovetail. ECJ can be used to optimize ABM models in parallel, which are then assessed on-the-fly in MASON. MASON also has extension libraries for social networks and for 2D rigid body kinematics, among other tools.

Finally but critically, D-MASON [13] extends MASON into a distributed model toolkit intended to run over a large number of machines. When developing D-MASON, the University of Salerno chose MASON as its target platform largely because of its emphasis on ease of extensibility.

Coding Style. MASON was written in Java because ECJ was in Java. This is not a controversial decision: Ascape, Repast, and NetLogo also target the Java Virtual Machine. Java has enabled MASON to be portable, provide replicable code, and be efficient. But MASON lacks certain hallmarks of modern Java, such as generics, annotations, and lambdas. Some of this is cargo-cult programming, but much of it is due to efficiency considerations. For example, MASON has a special replacement for `java.util.ArrayList`, because until recently ArrayList's *get()*, *set()*, and *add()* methods had flaws which prevented them from being inlined. HotSpot has since worked around these errors, and so going forward we may adopt ArrayList, along with similar workarounds obviated by recent Java improvements.

4   Where Is MASON Going?

Taking a critical look at MASON, there are many opportunities for improvement. It is now over 15 years old, and was originally developed for Java 1.3, and so has warts and misfeatures stemming from its age. While reasonably high performance, it is also still fundamentally a non-distributed toolkit. And it is missing important functionality, such as good statistics tools, a testing facility, and so on. Going forward, we will be making many improvements to the system.

In 2013 we organized an NSF-sponsored workshop [20] that proposed nine community recommendations for how MASON could be enhanced to assist in cutting edge research in the future:

1. Give MASON better external language support and plugins for integrated development environments (IDEs).

2. Add advanced output and statistics architectures.
3. Add parallel and distributed facilities.
4. Upgrade MASON to reflect recent Java language changes.
5. Add a testing regimen.
6. Identify facilities to make MASON more useful to the science and technology education community.
7. Add collaborative archives for the MASON community to share models.
8. Add automated validation and parameter sweeping.
9. Improve MASON's GIS support and integrate it with distributed capabilities.

After the workshop, we applied for and received a three-year NSF grant (1727303) to improve MASON along these lines, and are now in its second year. Following the recommendations above, our plans to improve MASON fall into four areas. First, we are making MASON *more robust*. Second, we are building a *distributed* version of the software (including distributed GIS support) that runs over MPI on cloud computing platforms. Third, we are adding a variety of tools to make MASON more *friendly to coders*. Fourth, we intend to make MASON more *friendly to the ABM community* at large. We discuss these goals below.

4.1   Making MASON More Robust

Like much open source research software, MASON was built with few tests or automated quality control checks. Fortunately MASON has exhibited few serious bugs over the years, but it badly needs a testing harness. This is an interesting challenge for stochastic models because of the semi-random nature of the results generated. When results differ from expected results, is this because of a bug (or bug-fix) or is it due to the vagaries of the random number generator?

We are constructing a test harness that will run MASON through a battery of parameters and compare them with expected outputs. This will take advantage of MASON's replicability such that, given a fixed set of parameters and random number generator seeds, the outputs should be identical. We are building unit tests for MASON, and are devising stochastic distribution-based tests using common MASON models. These tests will be run many times over a large number of random number generator seeds. If changes cause distributions (mean, variance, etc.) to deviate significantly, this will raise a flag.

4.2   Making MASON Distributed

This task will consume the majority of our efforts over the next few years, and entails an integrated distributed model facility, distributed and improved GIS, and both large- and small-scale model optimization and validation. To support massively scaled agent-based models, we want MASON to take advantage of many compute cores by distributing agents and allowing them to run in parallel. The potentially high degree of coupling (due to arbitrary and dense agent-agent interaction) in ABM scenarios like social networks poses a challenge to distributed simulation as the interprocess communication can overwhelm the work done on individual cores. However many ABM models are distributed spatially, which can be straightforwardly distributed. We will target distributed spatial scenarios but aim to make it possible to distribute social networks, etc. when feasible.

We also recognize that distributing simulations presents a *brittle abstraction* to the model developer: to achieve increasing speedups, he generally must cater more and more to the specifics of the underlying distribution system. Many modelers will not wish to do this. Our goal will be to provide multiple API layers, whereby a modeler can choose to make his model distributed with few changes to the original, or (if he wishes) delve deeper into the details of distributed simulation in order to achieve higher performance.

Approach. Our work builds on D-MASON, which partitions the simulation space into regions, and assigns to agents in each region a *worker* to manage their scheduling, migration, and regional synchronization. A multicast channel (or *topic*) is assigned to each region, and workers subscribe to topics associated with the regions that overlap with their interest areas in order to receive relevant messages. Although D-MASON is an important first step towards a distributed MASON, it uses a simple space partitioning approach that is efficient for local communication, but inefficient for global communication.

The new distributed version of MASON maintains much of the publish-subscribe approach of D-MASON. Our current efforts are based on Parallel Discrete Event Simulation (PDES), a robust and scalable approach for distributed situation [12]. A PDES simulation consists of a distributed set of *logical processes* (LPs) executing in parallel. LPs generate events that often need to be processed by other LPs. The LP abstraction provides a clean and modular method for achieving scalable performance.

Two major components in MASON's distributed architecture are data sharing between LPs and load balancing. In terms of data sharing, in distributed MASON, the simulation field is partitioned into several axis-aligned (hyper)rectangular regions. Each LP holds one region and processes all the agents that are located in that region. The basic idea is to assign, when possible, each LP its own CPU core. For performance reasons we use peer-to-peer message passing via MPI.

We recognize that highly connected graphs, such as may be found in social networks, impose a strong coupling between distributed nodes, resulting in heavy use of network resources. As a result we have chosen to focus on the more easily distributed case: spatially distributed models. Distribute MASON will also support networks, but not necessarily with efficiency guarantees.

In most spatially distributed models MASON agents often need to access nearby data, known as their *area of interest* (AOI). To support quick access of data within the AOI, each LP not only stores the data in its own region, but also maintains a cache of some data from its neighbors, called the *halo area*. Part of the LP's own data is cached by its neighbor LPs. This cache is called the *shared area*. The sizes of these two areas are defined by AOI. After each simulation step, each LP will pull the data from its neighbors into its halo area and at the same time send the data in the shared area to its corresponding neighbors, in a process called *halo exchange*. Access of data outside an agent's AOI is supported via remote procedure calls (RPCs) between LPs. Data is provided in a synchronous fashion, meaning the caller will get the value once the RPC call returns.

Load balancing among active processors, where each LP tries to balance the workload among its immediate members, is critical for performance. This is done as follows. Each node measures its runtime every step, and when a node performs load-balancing, it collects the runtimes from its neighbors. Based on the runtimes, it chooses a neighbor and expands or shrinks its region such that the variance of runtimes among the node and its neighbors is minimized. For speed in making load-balancing decisions, we assume the runtime is linear in the size of the region.

Each partition adjustment can only shift the border by at most its own AOI to avoid additional data exchange between nodes, since each node already has part of its neighbors' data in its halo area. This restriction might seem to slow down the load balancing, but we think that this is preferable because by limiting the adjustment and avoiding additional data exchange, the overhead is minimized and therefore the local load balancing can be done more frequently, better adapting to the change in workload. Another optimization is to avoid expensive coordination and synchronization activities by not allowing two neighboring LPs to perform load-balancing at the same time. To enforce this, we have implemented a graph coloring algorithm in the system so that at each step only the LPs with a designated color may balance their loads with neighbors.

Purely local load balancing runs the risk of getting caught in a local optimum. For this reason we plan to implement a hybrid local-global load balancing policy, using a hierarchy of LPs in a tree-structure, such as a K-D tree or a Quad Tree.

Distributed GIS Support. As part of making MASON distributed, it is crucial to also make GeoMASON distributed. However GIS presents unique and difficult challenges. Geospatial data generally comes in *raster* (grid) or *vector* form. GeoMASON raster data maps straightforwardly to MASON grid data structures and so is easy to apply in a distributed fashion. But vector data can span large areas: for example, assuming we are distributing spatially, a river or a road might span our entire network of machines. We tackle this by breaking the vector data into three kinds. Point data can be easily distributed using standard MASON data structures. Most non-point data is static and immutable (roads, rivers): we can simply give copies of it to every single processor. Finally, *mutable non-point* data is typically static and ideally less common, so we may distribute it with the non-point data but embed each such object with a pointer to a secondary object located on a specific (distributed) machine where mutable information is held.

Distributed Optimization, Automated Model Validation, and Parameter Sweeping. A major challenge faced by multiagent simulation is the complexity of validating models. MAS involves many heterogeneous variables, agents, agent behaviors, and interactions, and the model developer only knows the proper settings for some of these. To validate the model, one must optimize the remaining variables so as to match known ground truth, a laborious task. Model validation is often an optimization problem: the researcher hunts for parameter settings resulting in a model with low output error, and which is insensitive to certain parameters.

As a massively parallel stochastic optimization tool, ECJ is designed for exactly this task: the researcher defines known parameters and their values, then optimizes the remaining variables by running many models in parallel on back-end machines. MASON was designed from the ground-up to work with ECJ in this regard, but at present the two can be integrated only with considerable knowledge of both. We are working to make using MASON + ECJ for validation as simple as writing some code to assign a fitness to a simulation result, and then pressing a button on the MASON GUI. This is possible because MASON models are entirely self-contained and serializable. When a model is started, it is presented with a vector of parameters to use, and when it is done, it returns an *assessment* of the resulting run. ECJ will do the rest of the work.

Another common modeling task is sensitivity analysis. To address this, we will soon be releasing a parameter-sweep facility in MASON in which you can specify independent and dependent variables, then do parameter sweeps through the independent variables while logging dependent variable results. This is available in other tools (such as NetLogo): our goal is to initially permit parallelism and ultimately cloud distribution of the simulations during the sweep.

4.3   Making MASON More Coder-Friendly

IDE Support. We are building MASON tools for Eclipse, and potentially NetBeans. First, we are adding *code templates* that allow users to generate code skeletons for common MASON patterns. The goal is to reduce the drudgery in dealing with MASON's high degree of boilerplate. Second, we are adding several *wizards* that walk the user through the process of creating a model, where he can choose from common model scenarios, parameters, and visualization options, and finally generate easily modifiable model code. We currently have this working in-house.

External Language Support. A common request has been to provide some degree of external language support for MASON, particularly for languages which target the Java virtual machine (such as Jython, Scala, Clojure, and so on). This is not difficult given that these languages have Java function call support. But the primary difficulty is that many of these languages are slow in accessing Java data directly, as they would need to do when working with MASON. We can at least provide API support for the languages as a first step, then consider how we might encapsulate common ABM coding patterns in MASON utility functions so as to spend as much of the application runtime on the pure-Java side, where it is often much more efficient. We have proof-of-concept support for several languages.

Output and Statistics. MASON can make charts and graphs and track variables in the GUI, but does not have library support to output statistics. We are remedying this. We think the best way for an experimenter to do this is to have MASON dump statistics into files designed to be directly entered into a tool such as *R* [6]. But we will also consider integrating well-vetted implementations of basic statistical analyses, such as descriptive statistics, difference tests, and confidence intervals, perhaps from a library such as Apache Commons Math [2].

4.4   Making MASON More Community-Friendly

Collaborative Archives and Facilities. One major goal in MASON is to allow people to easily distribute and collaborate on public models. We presently offer several ways to do this, including a contributions section in the MASON repository. However, we want to go further. We hope to develop a special online repository to enable researchers to distribute models as `jar` files. We are exploring how to enhance MASON to advertise available models from this repository and enable users to download and run them (taking a cue from similar facilities such as in NetBeans). This would enable researchers to distribute models more easily, and also give educators and new users immediate access to a large and useful collection of educational demos and tutorials.

Education Aids and Examples. Building on the collaborative archive and improved external language support, we hope to make MASON friendlier to science and engineering education by extending MASON's GUI to be more friendly to beginning users, creating a "simple" restricted Java API to MASON for students to use in lieu of the full API (for building simple models), and adding a significant number of new educational examples drawn from several disciplines.

4.5   Development Plan

Our three-year development plan is as follows. In all three years we will develop distributed MASON and distributed GIS facilities. In the first year we have also focused on automated model validation and GUI facilities. In the second year we will work on the test harness and unit and integration tests, as well as the collaborative archive. In the final year we will work on statistics utilities, external language support, and educational aids.

5   Conclusion

Since its introduction in 2003 MASON has proven to be a successful open-source agent-based modeling toolkit, with a particular emphasis on high performance, flexibility, and ease of customization. But MASON can be improved in many areas, including making it fully distributed, adding optimization and sensitivity analysis, and making the tool more friendly to newcomers. These plans are ambitious but achievable, and we hope that they will serve to make MASON a strong foundation for ABM development over the next decade.

A critical part of this project is ABM community involvement. We are forming a group of MASON power-users and critics to help us revise our approach, and we invite interested modelers and developers to participate in the effort.

Acknowledgments. MASON's development team has included Sean Luke, Gabriel Catalin Balan, Keith Sullivan, Liviu Panait, Haoliang Wang, Ermo Wei, David Freelan, Sean Paus, Daniel Kuebrich, Joey Harrison, Paul Wiegand, Maciej Latek, and Ankur Desai, with support from Claudio Cioffi-Revilla. MASON's rigid-body kinematics package was developed by Christian Thompson. GeoMASON was developed by Mark Coletti and Keith Sullivan. D-MASON was developed by Carmine Spagnuolo, Vittorio Scarano, and Gennaro Cordasco. Thanks also to James Olds, Dan Rogers, Ken De Jong.

GMU modelers who helped stress-test MASON include Bill Kennedy, Jeff Bassett, Brian Hrolenok, Atesmachew Hailegiorgis, Tim Gulden, Katherine Russell, Tony Bigbee, Mark Rouleau, Sarah Wise, Guillermo Calderón Meza, Lance Sherry, and Rob Axtell. Thanks also to our many international users and testers.

MASON has been supported by grants from NSF, DARPA, ONR, the US Army, and the Naval Research Laboratory; most via recently NSF Grant 1727303.

References

1. Ascape agent-based modeling toolkit. http://ascape.sourceforge.net/
2. Commons Math. http://commons.apache.org/proper/commons-math/
3. ECJ metaheuristics library. http://cs.gmu.edu/~eclab/projects/ecj/
4. FLAME multiagent simulation tool. http://www.flame.ac.uk
5. NetLogo simulation platform. http://ccl.northwestern.edu/netlogo/
6. The R project for statistical computing. http://www.r-project.org/
7. Repast agent-based modelling toolkit. https://repast.github.io/
8. Repast HPC large-scale modeling platform. https://repast.github.io/
9. SWARM agent-based simulation toolkit. http://www.swarm.org/
10. Axtell, R.: Social science as computation. Technical report, Center for Economic and Social Dynamics, Brookings Institution, Washington, DC (2001)
11. Bassett, J.K., De Jong, K.A.: Evolving behaviors for cooperating agents. In: Raś, Z.W., Ohsuga, S. (eds.) ISMIS 2000. LNCS (LNAI), vol. 1932, pp. 157–165. Springer, Heidelberg (2000). https://doi.org/10.1007/3-540-39963-1_17
12. Boukerche, A., Lu, K.: Optimized dynamic grid-based DDM protocol for large-scale distributed simulation systems. In: IEEE International Parallel and Distributed Processing Symposium (2005)
13. Chiara, R.D., Mancuso, A., Mazzeo, D., Scarano, V., Spagnuolo, C.: Bringing together efficiency and effectiveness in distributed simulations: the experience with D-MASON. Simul. Trans. Soc. Model. Simul. Int. (2013)
14. Cioffi-Revilla, C., et al.: MASON NorthLands: a geospatial agent-based model of coupled human-artificial-natural systems in boreal and arctic regions. In: European Social Simulation Association (ESSA) (2015)
15. Crooks, A.T., Hailegiorgis, A.B.: An agent-based modeling approach applied to the spread of cholera. Environ. Model. Softw. **62**, 164–177 (2014)

16. Enright, J.J., Wurman, P.R.: Optimization and coordinated autonomy in mobile fulfillment systems. In: AAAI Workshop on Automated Action Planning for Autonomous Mobile Robots (2011)
17. Epstein, J.M., Axtell, R.: Growing Artificial Societies: Social Science From the Bottom Up. MIT Press, Cambridge (1996)
18. Gilbert, N., Troitzsch, K.G.: Simulation for the Social Scientist. Open University Press, Berkshire (1999)
19. Parker, L.E.: The effect of heterogeneity in teams of 100+ mobile robots. In: Multi-Robot Systems Volume II: From Swarms to Intelligent Automata, pp. 205–215. Kluwer (2003)
20. Payette, N., et al.: Future MASON directions: community recommendations (report of the 2013 MASON NSF workshop). Technical report, GMU-CS-TR-2013-9, Department of Computer Science, George Mason University (2013)
21. Sullivan, K., Luke, S.: Learning from demonstration with swarm hierarchies. In: Proceedings of the 11th International Conference on Autonomous Agents and Multiagent Systems (AAMAS) (2012)
22. Sullivan, K., Wei, E., Squires, B., Wicke, D., Luke, S.: Training heterogeneous teams of robots. In: Autonomous Robots and Multirobot Systems (ARMS) (2015)

American vs German Teams: The Case of Human Resources Consumption

Nuno Trindade Magessi[(✉)] and Luis Antunes[(✉)]

Faculdade de Ciências/BioISI – Biosystems and Integrative Sciences Institute,
Universidade de Lisboa, Lisbon, Portugal
nmaggessi@hotmail.com, xarax@ciencias.ulisboa.pt

Abstract. Teams are compulsive consumers of human resources from companies. This type of resources has associated the spending of money. There are two distinct types of teams: American and German. These two highly distinct models have specific characteristics that shape their patterns and dynamics. One characteristic that has been understudied in the literature is the resources consumption. To understand this issue, a multi-agent based model was developed to analyse each type of teams according to specific and critical aspects. After several simulations, it could be observed that German teams despite their focus on efficiency, were more compulsive consumers of human resources than American ones. The article also looks at hybrid teams where companies have a mix of both models. These teams tended to display more similarities with the German rather than the American model.

1 Introduction

Hyper competition means that companies must maximise their capacity to innovate [1, 2]. This need is more than just the urge to create new and innovative products. It is the fundamental need for survival that comes before any attempt to keep ahead of the competition. Innovation is the key to survival and the central tool for innovation is knowledge [3, 4]. Companies are made up of people and, in analogy to Darwin [5], companies who survive aggressive competition are not necessarily the strongest but those who best adapt to market mutations and the needs they create. The successful ones are those who adapt their behaviours, working methods, processes and come up with new ideas. Group is structured into teams, which are typically egocentric. They typically compulsively absorb as many company resources as possible.

Teams result from the need to gather together individuals with different ideas, skills, and resources [6]. Creativity is spurred when proven innovations in one domain are introduced into new ones, solving old problems and inspiring fresh thinking [7–10]. However, research shows that the right balance of diversity on teams is elusive. Although diversity may potentially spur creativity, it typically promotes conflict and miscommunication [11, 12]. It also runs counter to the safety most individuals feel when working and sharing ideas with past collaborators [13]. Successful teams evolve toward a size that is large enough to enable specialization and effective division of labour among teammates but small enough to avoid overwhelming costs of group coordination [14]. Unsuccessful teams become, by nature, an exaggerated consumer of

© Springer Nature Switzerland AG 2019
P. Davidsson and H. Verhagen (Eds.): MABS 2018, LNAI 11463, pp. 87–98, 2019.
https://doi.org/10.1007/978-3-030-22270-3_7

resources. This article analyses two different models of team management, the American and the German, in terms of resources consumption. To tackle this problem, a multi-agent model was designed where agents established collaboration through networks illustrating how the behaviour of individuals in assembling small teams for short-term projects can give rise to a variety of large-scale network structures which are absorbers of resources over time.

This article is organised as follows: in the next section, reviews the relevant literature about team building and the characteristics of the two models in terms of their impact on resources consumption. Section 3 describes the multi-agent model that was developed to analyse this issue. Section 4 displays the obtained results. Finally, in Sect. 5, we discuss our conclusions and make suggestions for future research.

2 Team Assembly Overview

Analyses of social networks are suggested as a tool for linking micro and macro levels of team building [7]. There are macro implications of one aspect of small-scale interaction: the strength of dyadic ties [7]. Sometimes there is a positive correlation between the degree of the overlap among individuals' friendship and the strengths of their ties to each other [7]. This has an impact on the sharing of influence and information as well as on opportunities for mobility and team organisation.

Team building has received a lot attention in terms of their capacity to change organisational environments especially uncertain ones. A review of team effectiveness literature reveals markedly different approaches and a lack of common ideas. There are numerous mentions of problems with teams in regards to inefficiency as well as their occasional inability to achieve targets [14].

Studies of work teams in a variety of organizational settings have shown that team effectiveness can be not hindered due to the absorption of resources from organisational structures which often replicate them (processes duplication) and end up serving as a source of conflict [7, 11–14].

Most of team assembly fails in some critical points enabled by structural features such as a well-designed team task, appropriate team composition, and a context that ensures the availability of information, resources, and rewards [14]. Many researchers have concluded that structure and design, including equipment, materials, physical environment, and pay systems, are the most important variables affecting work-team performance and respective improvement [7, 14]. An eventual lack of team success is not due to interpersonal factors [6, 7, 14]. Instead and according to these authors, organisation and team structures explain most of the variance in team effectiveness.

However, individuals' tacit beliefs about interpersonal interaction inhibit learning behaviour and give rise to organisational ineffectiveness [7].

The described factors explain the failure of organisations to adapt rationally due to cognitive biases that favour existing routines over alternatives. Once more, the case is conceived without any multiplier effect. Teams grow up to camouflage the ineffectiveness's of traditional organisational structures [7, 12, 14]. Their members tend to behave and engage in tough negotiations or fighting, as they try to obtain resources and processes that might allow them to adapt and improve.

Researchers are becoming more interested in group and team processes across cultures [15]. One key issue is to analyse the differences between American and German models of teams. The American model is more qualitative and its main focus is on achieving results and the subsequent effectiveness of the teams [15, 16]. The German model, however is more quantitative and focuses on choosing the right path and processes related to team efficiency. Another difference is the fact that Americans do not track team records. In contrast, Germans record everything done by their teams in order to understand where efficiency improvements are needed [16, 17]. The American model always questions the processes unleashed by their teams. Americans can simply tear up everything related to a team and start all over again, when things go wrong, and results are not achieved. For Germans, the technique is different. They need to rebuild the process step-by-step to identify where the mistake occurred or problem under the auspices of the logic. The American model is based on an open door system that allows people to carry out any function for which they have the relevant competences, while the German one is more closed door [15, 16].

American teams are fast and creative and are built to conquer all the territory surrounding them. When problems arise, however, no one knows why, because they lack records. Germans, on the other hand, follow a logical method and they are built to achieve command over everything.

Earlier research also identified five other dimensions where American and Germans teams differed [17], namely power distance, uncertainty avoidance, collectivism versus individualism, gender and long versus short term orientation.

"Uncertainty avoidance refers to how people in a culture cope with the unpredictable and the ambiguous, how they deal with a lack of knowledge about the future, and to what extent they experience fear of the unknown" [15, 17].

Cultures differ in terms of avoiding or tolerating uncertainty. Uncertainty avoidant cultures tend to believe that what is different is dangerous, and have developed ways to mitigate uncertainty and potential anxiety about the future. For example, in organisational structures, important elements of uncertainty avoidance include the use of technology, rules, and rituals [17].

German teams tend to avoid uncertainty (cultural feature) and demonstrate a need to determine the future and to avoid risk [15]. On other hand, American teams often show less need to avoid uncertainty. People with there are more comfortable taking risks, since they have great confidence in their capacity to succeed in the future [15, 17].

In terms of behaviour, American teams may spend less time analysing problems and may produce quick solutions, whereas Germans teams are more likely to carefully analyse problems to figure out where they failed and critically evaluate possible alternatives [17].

In collective cultures, teams tend to value consensus and loyalty over individual inventiveness, whereas in individualistic cultures, each team member's ideas are deemed important, so teams encourage expression of original ideas. While both, the American and German, approaches are described as individualists, the latter are much less so [15, 17]. There is also more specialisation in the case of American model than in German one model where multi-tasking is more common.

Another important dimension is team orientation. In such case, American teams are generally more solution oriented in order to achieve targets, whereas German teams often focus more on problem analysis [15]. Thus, it is natural that German teams have more probability to concentrate their efforts on gathering precise details and as much information as possible.

These considerations have not yet dealt with the importance of resource consumption, which will be addressed by the model developed for this purpose.

3   The Team Building Model

The Team Building Model (TBM) is a multi-agent model built using Netlogo software [18] in order to analyse which model uses the greater quantity of resources, thereby creating more problems for their teams. This model provides us the dimension for each team and the complexity that was established among the agents.

This model of team building illustrates how the behaviour of agents when putting together small teams for projects may use up extreme quantities of human resources over time as a result of high complexity of their organisational structures. The model is an adaptation of the team assembly model [6, 19].

3.1   TBM Model Parameters

The Team Building Model is composed of a set of parameters that characterises some aspects of team models. The model is split into the parameters that affect all types of agents.

a. Team-Size: the number of agents in a newly assembled team.
b. Max-Leisure: the number of runs an agent will not be call to work before retirement.
c. ρ: the probability of an inexperienced resource from outside the company is chosen to become a member of a new team.
d. ς: the probability that the team being assembled will include a previous collaborator who has worked on the team, given that the team has at least one resource allocated.
e. δ: the probability of an agent being individualistic. Of course $(1 - \delta)$ represents the probability of an agent being collectivistic
f. υ: the probability that an agent is uncertainty avoidant. Alternative $(1 - \upsilon)$ is the likelihood that an agent is not uncertainty avoidant.
g. φ: the probability of an agent being a problem solver; $(1 - \varphi)$ represents agents who are not a problem solver.

The combination of these parameters allows researchers to represent two distinct models: the American and the German, being represented by [20%–80%] or [80%–20%] depending on which model we are dealing with. Nevertheless, it was simulated the hybrid case [50%–50%] to analyse what happens in terms of resources consumption. Hybrid cases happen when groups intentionally use that part of each model that better fits their own interests (see Fig. 1).

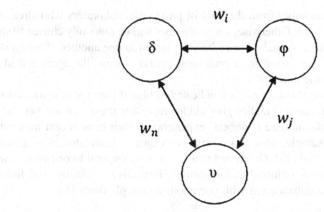

Fig. 1. The combination of parameters with respective weights w_i, w_j and w_n generated randomly to identify if the agent is American or German.

The option for these combinations is that it is rare to form a team that is composed solely and exclusively of elements that have as reference one of these two types of model. The personality, not addressed in the scope of this article is a determining factor. The percentages presented represent agents with a German, American and hybrid (mixed) culture in the team composition and used in the simulations, to see which of the predominant scenarios reflects the management culture model that consumes more human resources.

Obviously one can ask, if it should not be [100%–0%], the inverse and [50%–50%]? The answer is that, in reality, the probability that, in a team, there is no one with a different culture is low. Hence that composition was used where the great majority of the agents is from one or the other model of culture and to test if a mix of both can reduce the consumption of human resources by a team. This mix is no more than the Japanese model that at the level of efficiency resembles the German, but after the Second World War was greatly influenced by the American model.

3.2 Explaining TBM Model

Most of the general features and human resources consumption could be found in the networks established among team members inside the companies. These general features can be captured by the Team Assembly model with two simple parameters: the proportion of newcomers participating in a team and the propensity for past collaborators to work again with one another [6]. However, this model went a step further and we added more parameters in order to check which cultural team model consumed a greater degree of resources.

At each tick a new team member is assembled. Team members are either inexperienced team workers (people who have not previously participated in any type of teams) or are experienced team workers. Each member is chosen sequentially. The ρ slider gives the probability that an outsider will be an inexperienced team worker. If the new member is not inexperienced, then with a probability given by the ς slider, a trainee will be chosen randomly from the pool of previous collaborators who already have participated on the team. Otherwise, a new member will be randomly chosen from all trainees. When a team is created, all members are linked to one another. If an agent does not participate in a new team for a prolonged period of time, the agent and his links are removed from the network.

Agents in newly "assembled teams" are indicated in blue if they are new members and yellow if they are trainees. Smaller grey circles represent those that are not currently collaborating. Links indicate members' experience at their most recent moment of collaboration. For example, blue links between agents indicate that two agents collaborated as new members [6]. Green and yellow links correspond to one-time new member-trainee and among trainees' collaborations, respectively. Finally, red links indicate that agents have collaborated with one another multiple times [6].

- **Blue**: two new members;
- **Green**: a new member and a trainee;
- **Yellow**: two trainees who have not previously collaborated together;
- **Red**: Repeated members.

The model counts the number of links established in the collaboration among the team over time. It outputs the percentage of agents in a mega structure. This output

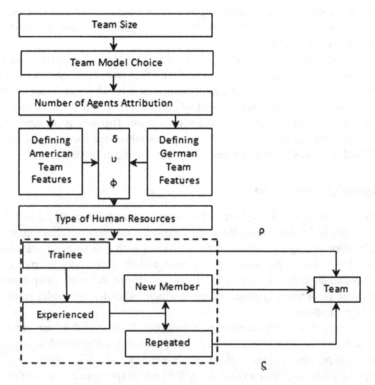

Fig. 2. TBM Model explanation of the relation between parameters and agent' types

variable gives us the extent and the use of human resources by a team. It also plots the percentage of agents belonging to the largest team over time (see Fig. 2).

A team with a big structure is defined by the number of agents forming the teams. For example, if in the 1st run the agent system generates a team with 2 elements, in the 2nd adds another getting 3 agents. In the 3rd run a team of 6 elements is formed and in the 4th run a team of 8 elements. However, if in the 5th run the agent system generates a team or several teams with only 3 elements, but without connection to each other, then the agent system retains the one that had more agents, as the largest team.

Meanwhile, the larger team can continue with all its elements or disaggregate depending on the combination of parameters and probability. If the large structure holds and adds more elements, the percentage of agents in a team with a large structure corresponds to a fraction of the number of agents in that run that are part of the big team upon the maximum number of agents that belonged to that structure.

Now, for the percentage to increase, it is because the numerator increases and the denominator considered decreases. If the percentage decreases it means that the team had for example a maximum of 10 elements, but in the following runs the number of agents belonging to that team decreased. In the situation where there is training of several teams, is the maximum weighted average of the teams that is considered for calculation purposes.

On the other hand, the average team size gives the dimension of isolated collaboration teams as a fraction of the total number of agents. If we analyse the plots dynamics, we can observe important features of the team, such as the distribution of link types or how the connectivity of the team varies over time.

The TBM model portrays, on one hand, the distribution type of the connections among team members. An overabundance of new member-new member (**blue**) links might indicate that a field is not taking advantage of experienced members. On the other hand, a multitude of repeated collaborations (**red**) and trainees-trainees (**yellow**) links may indicate a lack of diversity in ideas or experience.

On the other hand, there is the overall connectivity of team collaboration. We can also see the different emergent topologies appear in the display. New collaborations or synergy among teams naturally tends to the center of the display. Teams or clusters of teams with few connections to new collaborations naturally "float" to the edges of the "world". New members always start in the center of it. Randomly chosen trainees may be located in any part of the screen. Thus, collaborations amongst new members and or distant team members tend toward the center, while disconnected clusters are repelled.

Furthermore, the agents who will incorporate the team are set up in the center and float to "out" as a result of team expansion. This entire model's procedure is generated randomly depending on where the activity is launched and position further away if they are less risk averse to more individualistic and more problem solver or more autonomous.

In the simulation the teams can vary depending on the combinations formed by the parameters referring to the, also variable, probabilities. What I mean is that teams are generated according to the evolution of the combination of parameters and attributes of the agents. That is generated by the template. The team can aggregate itself and then evolve to disaggregate according to the probabilities. Thus, the decision to add an element to the team derives from its characterization and is generated automatically by the system itself. In this way it is the system that decides per se if it adds another element or elements to the team, if it dispenses them disintegrating the existing team or if it keeps the team as it is. The objective of each team is always to solve a certain activity of an abstract project.

On the other hand, the measures that are taken to allow the performance evaluation and make a new decision, once again, depend on the combination's evolution of the parameters of the model.

Each of the agent's probabilities is generated using a random-float function during the simulation, both for trainees and experienced. And when that probability is greater than p (that works like a threshold and controlled, at the interface, by us) along with the fact that there is no experienced member available in the market (netlogo world), the trainee is recruited. If there are experienced human resources on the market and the probability generated at random by it is greater than ç, then it has priority over the rest (see Fig. 3).

But before that, regardless of whether it is a trainee or an experienced human resource, if the team has a Germanic model, only agents with the probabilities (listed in the parameters) that fit the German work profile enters the team. Or, in the American model, agents that present a probability (generated randomly for each agent as attribute) closer to the American style, fixed by the parameters that define the agent typology, like gamma, v and phi.

$$\begin{cases} p_{experienced} & , if\ random-float\ p_{experienced} > \varsigma \\ p_{trainee}\ , if\ random-float\ p_{trainee} > p\ and \sim p_{experienced}\ v\ p_{experienced} = 0 \end{cases}$$

Fig. 3. Agent's probabilities restrictions

Finally, it must be pointed out that the structure of team collaboration in the model can change dramatically over time. Initially, only new teams are generated; the collaborative field has not existed long enough for members to retire. However, after a period of time (Max-Leisure), inactive agents begin to retire, and the number of agents becomes relatively stable – the emergent effects of ρ and ç become more apparent at this equilibrium stage. Note also that the end of the growth stage is often marked by a drop in team connectivity.

In short, the purpose of the agent model is to know primarily which of the models, American or German, to perform an activity, consumes or has a greater need for more human resources. This activity is abstract and that awakens the beginning of the team.

4   Simulation Results and Analysis

The results reported in this section were obtained conducting the described experiments using version 5.0.4 of the NetLogo framework [18]. NetLogo is a programmable modelling environment for simulating natural and social phenomena. It is particularly well suited for modelling complex systems and developing them over time.

At this stage, I will limit myself to the analysis defined by the scope of this article. I will present the obtained results, and the respective analysis.

4.1 American Teams

First of all, we analysed the case of American teams. It can be seen that the percentage of agents in big team structures decreased throughout the simulation (see Fig. 4).

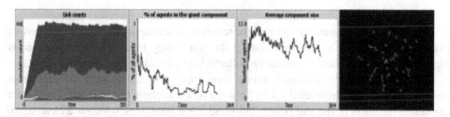

Fig. 4. American team building

Another important point is that the number of agents in a team grew exponentially from the beginning of the simulation until it reached a maximum of 12.8 members per team, when the standard team size was set in 4. The average number then started to decrease with a lot of volatility. As we can also observe that the American teams were more likely to conquer the space split in small teams with fewer links among them. They were more individualistic as was described by [15, 17].

Most links among team members can be seen to take place among new members, followed by those links established between new members and trainees. There was a little use of red links and a high use of blue ones, which clearly signaled the American preference for taking risks.

4.2 German Teams

In the case of the German teams, the percentage of agents in big team structures was constant during the simulation. The fact of the percentage of agents was constant means that in the predominantly German model the percentage of teams considered as large were constant, reaching the maximum in terms of their size. In other words, the team or teams increased the numerator and the denominator exponentially in the same proportion by setting a maximum number fixed at the beginning and this was constant. it results in a node knot that reflects the links between all the agents that emerged throughout the simulation. Human resources (agents) were fully, constantly and continuously used throughout. The same result could be seen regarding average team size. The average size increased gradually during the period of analysis and tended to remain near the top with an average of 12.3 team members (see Fig. 5).

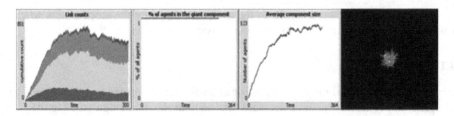

Fig. 5. German team building

Another important finding was that the teams used less space and did so at a greater level of concentration in the dominion of the space they have. These results clearly suggest that German teams were more collectivistic according the obtained results.

Most of the links established among team members can be seen to come from trainees, followed by those established between new members and trainees. There were substantial numbers of red and yellow links and fewer blue ones, which is a clear signal of the German preference to avoid risks, as predicted by the literature.

4.3 Hybrid Teams

In an add-on to this work, we can verify hybrid teams are a case between American and German models. These teams, did not utilise all available agents as did the German teams, but they are far from the values presented by the American teams. In sum, hybrid teams were more similar to German than American teams. The average number of team members fluctuated greatly during the simulation, reaching a maximum of 16.0 members per team (see Fig. 6).

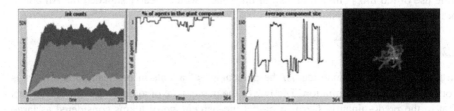

Fig. 6. Hybrid team building

It is also important to point out that Hybrid teams are more expansive in space than German teams but substantially less than American ones.

In terms of links among team members, we can observe that most arose from new members and trainees, followed by those established among new members. The existence of repeated collaborators was almost equal to that of German teams. So it seems these teams were more available to take risks than German teams, but substantially less likely to do so than the American teams.

5 Conclusion and Future Work

This work made use of the multi-agent based system methodology to develop a model to study and compare whether the American or German team building model would consume more resources. The obtained results revealed a couple of interesting findings. First of all, German teams clearly consumed more human resources than American ones. German teams had a preference for dominance and consumed a high level of resources in a kind of loop. Second, American teams had more propensity to take risks than German ones. Thirdly, American teams were more individualistic than German ones and had more propensity to conquer new spaces. German teams were more likely to establish links of control.

Finally, the hybrid teams are the cases between the American model and German one. However, this model has more similarities with German teams than the American ones. This suggests that to be an American team there was a need for more extreme parameters.

Future research will take in consideration the possibility of the different and new characteristics of teams, fundamentally regarding their purposes.

References

1. Geroski, P., Machin, S., Reenen, J.: The profitability of innovating firms. RAND J. Econ. **24**, 198–211 (1993)
2. Czarnitzki, D.: An empirical test of the asymmetric models on innovative activity: who invests more into R&D, the incumbent or the challenger? J. Econ. Behav. Organ. **54**, 153–173 (2004)
3. Grant, R.: Toward a knowledge-based theory of the firm. Strateg. Manag. J. **17**, 109–122 (1996)
4. McEvily, S., Chakravarthy, B.: The persistence of knowledge-based advantage: an empirical test for product performance and technological knowledge. Strateg. Manag. J. **23**, 285–305 (2002)
5. Darwin, C.R.: The Origin of Species. The Harvard Classics, vol. XI. P.F. Collier & Son 1909–14, New York (2001). Bartleby.com. www.bartleby.com/11/
6. Guimera, R., Uzzi, B., Spiro, J., Amaral, L.: Team assembly mechanisms determine collaboration network structure and team performance. Science **308**(5722), 697–702 (2005)
7. Granovetter, M.: The strengthen of weak ties. Am. J. Sociol. **78**, 1360 (1973)
8. Reagans, R., Zuckerman, E.: Networks, diversity, and productivity: the social capital of corporate R&D teams. Organ. Sci. **12**, 502 (2001)
9. Burt, R.: Structural Holes and Good Ideas. Am. J. Sociol. **110**, 349 (2004)
10. Uzzi, B., Spiro, J.: Collaboration and creativity: the small world problem. Am. J. Sociol. **111** (2), 447–504 (2005)
11. Larson, J., Christensen, C., Abbott, A., Franz, T.: Diagnosing groups: charting the flow of information in medical decision-making teams. J. Pers. Soc. Psychol. **71**, 315 (1996)
12. Edmondson, A.: Psychological safety and learning behavior in work teams. Adm. Sci. Q. **44**, 350 (1999)
13. Strasser, G., Stewart, D., Wittenbaum, G.: Expert roles and information exchange during discussion: the importance of knowing who knows what. J. Exp. Soc. Psychol. **31**, 244 (1995)

14. Katzenback, J., Smith, D.: The Wisdom of Teams - High Performance Teams. Harvard Business School Press, Harvard (1993)
15. Lehmann-Willenbrock, N., Allen, J.A., Meinecke, A.L.: Observing culture: differences in US-American and German team meeting behaviors. Group Processes Intergroup Relat. **17** (2), 252–271 (2014)
16. Tadmor, C.T., Satterstrom, P., Jang, S., Polzer, J.T.: Beyond individual creativity: the super additive benefits of multicultural experience for collective creativity in culturally diverse teams. J. Cross Cult. Psychol. **43**, 384–392 (2012). https://doi.org/10.1177/0022022111435259
17. Hofstede, G.: Culture's Consequences: Comparing Values, Behaviors, Institutions, and Organizations Across Nations, 2nd edn. Sage Publications, Thousand Oaks (2001)
18. Wilensky, U.: NetLogo. Center for Connected Learning and Computer-Based Modeling, Northwestern University, Evanston, IL (1999). http://ccl.northwestern.edu/netlogo/
19. Bakshy, E., Wilensky, U.: NetLogo Team Assembly Model. Center for Connected Learning and Computer-Based Modeling, Northwestern University, Evanston, IL (2007). http://ccl.northwestern.edu/netlogo/models/TeamAssembly

Simulation of Bank Transaction Data

Martin Mocko and Jakub Ševcech$^{(\boxtimes)}$

Faculty of Informatics and Information Technologies,
Slovak University of Technology in Bratislava,
Ilkovičova 2, 842 16 Bratislava, Slovakia
martin.mocko1@gmail.com, jakub.sevcech@stuba.sk

Abstract. When working with data such as financial transactions or user activity logs, in domains with inherent privacy concerns, you will certainly run into problems with data protection and data availability. Among possible approaches to cope with these problems are data anonymization and data simulation. One of essential advantages in favor of data simulation is complete separation from subject identification.

In this paper, we present a multi-agent simulation framework applicable in financial domain for transaction data generation. We use the framework to create multiple simulation scenarios reproducing typical fraudulent behavioral patterns and we evaluate its applicability on the task of Anti Money Laundering (AML) by classification of fraudulent agents.

Keywords: Multi-agent based simulation · Anti-money laundering · Transaction data

1 Introduction

In research and in practice as well, one of the most important necessities, to be able to make relevant conclusions, is data. Having complete data of good quality goes a long way in achieving the results that researchers strive for. However, in certain domains, getting access to the data can become a very arduous and complicated, if not impossible, task. One frequent obstacle is data privacy and protection concerns.

To cope with these problems, many methods for data anonymization were proposed: personal identification data removal, noise introduction into the data, granularity coarsening to ensure certain level of indistinguishability between observations (K-anonymity, L-diversity, T-closeness [1]), transformation into latent space using methods such as Principal Component Analysis, etc.

The common goal of all these approaches is to make it impossible to connect individuals with observations in the data and at the same time to preserve other data characteristics valuable for data analysis task at hand. Poorly anonymized dataset can lead to identification of individual observations and nullification of the effort such as in the well known case of New York taxi trips dataset[1].

---

[1] https://chriswhong.com/open-data/foil_nyc_taxi/.

© Springer Nature Switzerland AG 2019
P. Davidsson and H. Verhagen (Eds.): MABS 2018, LNAI 11463, pp. 99–114, 2019.
https://doi.org/10.1007/978-3-030-22270-3_8

One possibility, in order to completely separate personal information from valuable characteristics of a dataset, is to build a simulation based on original data properties for new dataset construction. In such a way, we have complete control over the properties of the dataset to be published and at the same time, no individual records are linked to created observations. In that way, even other related datasets can not be used to reveal the identity of concerned subjects as the identity is completely removed and only selected data properties are conserved. At the same time, such a simulation allows us to control the number of observations to be created and allows us to create scenarios for specific segments or patterns present in the data. We dive deeper into the pros and cons of data simulation in Sect. 2.

In this paper, we present a multi-agent simulation framework for transaction data creation, that allows to create simulations for various scenarios. Individual agent behavior can be controlled using distributions extracted from real data or by rules programmed into the body of the agent.

We demonstrate the utility of the framework by its application in anti-money laundering (AML). In the following sections, we analyze advantages and limitations of using simulated data for further data analysis (Sect. 2), we introduce the simulation framework (Sect. 3), we describe its application to simulate multiple common money-laundering scenarios (Sect. 4) and we evaluate its applicability by comparison of multiple common methods for fraudulent account classification on simulated data (Sect. 5).

2   Data Generation by Simulation

As mentioned earlier, simulation can be used to generate anonymized data. However, one should always know the benefits and pitfalls of such approach and be careful with drawing conclusions. As described in [8] data generation by simulation has its advantages, but also has its drawbacks.
Benefits of using simulated data:

- we can simulate scenarios that happen infrequently as long as we know how they look like,
- customer identification and privacy is not affected,
- datasets we generate can be made publicly available more easily,
- disclosure of results obtained on simulated data are not affected by privacy policies,
- different scenario parameters can be fully controlled by the researcher,
- we can reduce unbalanced data problem by generating high quantities of abnormal data and
- class labels are readily available.

Drawbacks connected to the usage of synthetic data:

- the generated data might not be representative or realistic and can contain biased information,

- it is difficult to build a realistic model due to the complexity of variables, parameters and processes that correctly represent the domain
- it is unknown whether we can transfer the learning from a simulated dataset to a real-world dataset and
- simulated suspicious data cannot be investigated further for improving the accuracy of the existing classification algorithms.

Authors of this analysis used synthetic data in AML research in domains of mobile money service [9] and in retail [10], but similar approaches are also used in other domains such as video-on-demand service [3], credit card theft [7] or energy consumption [6]. All of these works exploited the advantage that the simulated data does not usually contain much leaked information from real data that could be used for deanonymization purposes. Therefore, this data can usually be shared further in the research community without worrying about privacy concerns.

To create a more realistic simulation, one can enrich the agents' personal information using demographic information; thus, creating synthesized populations. The agents can be assigned attributes such as sex, age, education, income, life expectancy, disease risk, or network position [5]. Usually, surveys and census data are used as sources for synthesizing such personal information about agents.

MAB (multi-agent based) simulation has been utilized in other domains as well. Research into the characteristics of trading under conditions of a global market price and local individual market prices was done in [14]. Agents were given a goal of getting enough resources (food) to ensure their welfare. Some agents had excess amounts of these resources and could sell them and others had insufficient amounts and were therefore incentivized to buy. The answer to whether or not the "Big Wing" tactic was the right tactic to use in the Battle for Britain was given in [12]. Agents corresponded to the RAF or the Luftwaffe fighters. Various statistical approaches, such as PCA, ANOVA and ANCOVA, were used. MAB simulation has been successfully used for disease spread modeling as well. Results of the work in [13] indicate that the increase in mobility and application of different control policies has an influence on the increase of dengue fever cases, pointing to a causality relationship.

Multi-agent based simulation is a computation methodology often used in social sciences, biology and other areas of research. Its main advantages are behavior simulation and interaction between many autonomous agents in time [11]. Agents are objects which have their own rules and states, and behave accordingly to them in every step of the simulation. However their behavior does not need to be static, and could be evolving dynamically. The main benefit of using a MABS for our work is that from those specified agents' (micro) behaviors, there can arise an emergent, global macro behavior. We say that the simulation has an emergent property. The potential of a MAB simulation was best utilized for Scenario 3, where fraudster agents were not simply creating actions by drawing from random distributions, but they behaved according to their specified rules and to the resources that were available to them, with a certain degree of randomness.

For the AML domain, the fraudsters (or launderers/attackers) try to mimic the behavior of normal users as close as possible, while trying to maximize the amount of money laundered. That is, their behavior can change over time or according to some specific short-time circumstances that the account is in. With this in mind, we decided to build a multi-agent based simulator (MABS).

For the sake of getting relevant results, it is important that the simulation is set up the right way. From our experience there are three types of ways the simulation can be meaningfully set up:

- using extracted (aggregated) information from real data,
- using the knowledge of a domain expert – histograms, statistics, averages, shape of distribution, etc.,
- validation and feedback by a domain expert.

We proposed the simulation framework to simulate common AML scenarios based on rules about agent behavior. We do not use the framework to create realistic complex data but to simulate specific narrow cases/scenarios. The rules governing those scenarios were partially based on money laundering red flags descriptions[2] and partially using domain experts' feedback.

3   Financial Data Simulation Framework

This section describes the design requirements and decisions that we took in creating the simulator (simulation framework). The implementation itself is in Python 3 programming language and is built on MESA simulation framework[3].

We have built a multi-agent simulation where various types of agents can be connected and can interact with each other using simulated financial transactions. These transactions are logged in order to create the simulated transaction dataset.

A simplified class diagram for the most important classes of the framework is displayed in Fig. 1. The main entry for the simulation is the BankModel class that connects all components, initializes them and steps through the simulation.

The setup process is separated into three steps:

- agents generation,
- connection generation and
- operation generation.

An example of a sequence of calls of these operations along with classes of objects they are executed on are displayed in sequence diagram in Fig. 2.

We implemented two basic types of agents:

- Agents which pick transaction amount from a specific distribution and send it to a chosen agent from among its connection with a defined probability. These distributions have to be provided by a domain expert in the form of a random distribution or a histogram or can be learned from real data.

---

[2]   https://www.ffiec.gov/bsa_aml_infobase/pages_misc/red.htm.
[3]   https://github.com/projectmesa/mesa/.

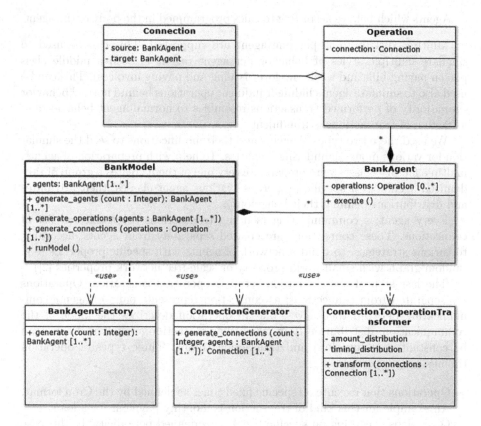

Fig. 1. Simplified class diagram of the simulation framework. The BankModel class is the main entry for the simulation.

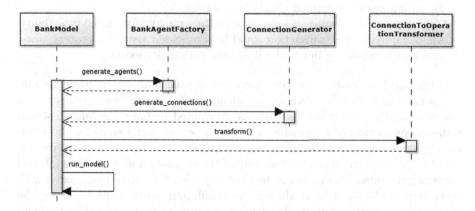

Fig. 2. An example of possible sequence of operations calls employed for simulation creation.

– Agents which behave according to rules programmed in the body of the agent.

Multiple distributions per one agent are supported. This can be used to simulate multiple styles of behavior per agent (agent is both a middle class person paying bills and a self-employer issuing and paying invoices). This can be used also to simulate agents hiding fraudulent operations behind normal behavior - a majority of performed transactions resembles to normal agent behavior and a fraction of transactions is fraudulent.

We used these two types of agents and their modifications to seed the simulation for various money laundering scenarios. To help with preparation of agents, multiple factory classes were prepared. Every one of them creates a group of randomized agents with specific properties (various agent classes, their attributes and distributions defining their behaviour).

Every agent is communicating (sending transactions to) a selected list of connections. These connections are created separately from agents, according to various strategies, to build a network of agents with specific properties (e.g. random graph with small world property or scale-free network properties [2]).

The last step of the simulation setup is operation generation. Operations are separated from connections; as connection represents pairs of agents communicating between themselves, but an operation describes the mode of the communication: distribution from which the transaction amount is drawn (can be constant or a function) and transaction timing. Three types of operation timings are supported:

– Operations that execute on specific fixed times as defined by the Cron format. An example for this kind of transaction is monthly payment for a loan.
– Operations executing on specific times with defined periodicity. In this case the operations are defined by a starting time and a periodicity length. An example for this transaction could be a repeated transaction with a custom time periodicity, which would mainly occur as a result of the bank account user using some automated transaction service.
– Operations that execute on some date or time range, given some probability. An example for this transaction could be a repeated visit to a grocery store. The visit is repeating but no hard defined periodicity exists.

Although the default time representation of such multi-agent based simulators usually are "steps", which are independent of any time measurement unit, this was insufficient for our use case as we wanted to meet the format of real transactions as closely as possible. Therefore, besides using steps for the simulation (where one step means every agent executes their behavior once), we also are able to set a time stamp of the start of the simulation and the time interval between two steps. This allows us to have a specific time stamp associated with every step of the simulation, during the simulation, so that the times for the transaction execution can be also defined in terms of time and not in terms of simulator steps. This simplifies the usage of simulator generated data greatly and makes the use of such simulator much more intuitive to the real world scenario.

This framework design is versatile and extensible (all prepared classes such as agents, operations, connection generators, factory classes are parameterizable and extensible). It can be extended and adapted for specific uses and allows us to create many types of scenarios.

4 Money-Laundering Scenarios Simulation

Regulated financial entities are required to report suspicious transactions by many government authorities. This responsibility requires them to be able to monitor and identify transactions, evaluate them in real time, and flag the ones that are suspicious. To identify frequent suspicious activities a list of red flags exists[4] as described by Federal Financial Institutions Examination Council (FFIEC). In our work, we created several simulation scenarios that generate transactions that represent normal behaviour and transactions that should alert these flags. Specifically, we chose "Structured or recurring, non-reportable transactions" flag to simulate suspicious activity.

Know Your Customer (KYC) methods based on population demographic are very important part of money laundering detection process, but we simplified population demography in this demonstration (as we focused on transaction data simulation) to agents' name generation based on 1990 Census data[5].

4.1 Scenario 1: Transactions Just Under the Reporting Limit

The first scenario we implemented using our framework was a "high transaction amount" scenario. This is a very simple AML scenario where the fraudsters are trying to launder as much money as possible by making many transactions just below the reporting threshold limit. If this limit was exceeded the bank would be legally obliged to report this transaction to the authorities, since a high amount of money is involved in a single cash transaction. As fraudsters try to stay as much "under the radar" as possible, they avoid these kinds of thresholds and reporting situations.

Normal agents perform some typical transactions such as paying the phone bill, water bill, paying for food and paying rent defined by a Gaussian distribution. The simulation was set up in such a way that we had 9,500 normal agents and 500 fraudsters, keeping the percentage of fraudsters at 5%. In reality, the percentage of fraudsters in banks is probably even lower than that. The transactions for normal users are generally going to be under the amount of 2,000. The reporting limit for the high cash transaction was set at 10,000. The fraudsters were, therefore, incentivized to make transactions in the higher thousands, up to 9,999. In this scenario, agents were drawing random numbers from a distribution, however they could also have a preprogrammed behavior according to which they make their transactions. This would make their behavior more dynamic, making it more in line with the multi-agent simulation vision.

---

[4] https://www.ffiec.gov/bsa_aml_infobase/pages_misc/red.htm.
[5] https://www.census.gov/topics/population/genealogy.html.

It should be obvious that when the distributions of transaction amounts for the two kinds of agents are so far away from each other, the accounts that are doing the fraud should be easily detectable as well. For the purposes of this paper, we chose to evaluate the "hardest" dataset that we could generate for this scenario. Our definition of "hardest" is that the means of the two distributions should be equal. That should sufficiently simulate the situation where fraudsters are trying to hide themselves between the normal users. In the hardest dataset, the transaction amount distributions for the two types of agents are not easily separable, and we can see that in the results. An example of simulated transaction amounts for an easily separable dataset and a harder one are displayed on Fig. 3.

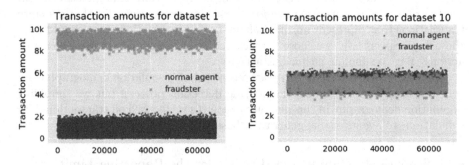

Fig. 3. Transaction amounts simulated for fraudsters and normal agents in scenario 1. Left figure shows distribution of the amounts for dataset 1 (easiest to classify). Right figure shows distribution of the amounts for dataset 10 (hardest to classify).

4.2   Scenario 2: Larger Amounts of Cash Deposits

The second scenario implemented using our simulation framework was a "larger amounts of cash deposits" scenario. Fraudster agents improved over the first scenario in a way that they would not create too many transactions with high transaction amounts. However, their main source of income is usually illegal. For this illegal trace to be associated with the money as little as possible, the fraudsters will usually receive larger payments in cash and then they will try to integrate the money into the financial system. Oftentimes they will pretend to be businesses for which it is common to receive larger amounts of payments in cash, such as car cleaning, restaurants or clothes cleaning.

The normal agents, again, perform their typical transactions as paying for the utilities, paying for rent, food, etc. They also perform deposit cash transactions, however, usually in much smaller amounts since most of the money they get is by wire. The fraudster agents pretend to do the same kind of transactions, however their main source of income is cash, and their deposits are bigger. The setup of the simulation was again, 9,500 normal agents and 500 fraudster agents. At first the fraudsters would make cash deposits of really high value, in the thousands. When the distributions of cash deposits for these two types of agents are very far away from each other, they are easily separable. Therefore, in order for the fraudsters to disguise themselves as normal agents, they had to lower the cash deposit amounts to the lower hundreds as to avoid much suspicion. That is how the "hardest" dataset was generated for this scenario. The fraudsters were making cash deposits practically indistinguishable in amount to the normal users. This also very much hinders their ability to launder a lot of money through the financial systems. They would generally seek other means how to get the cash into the system.

In this scenario, we focused on testing whether average monthly deposits and their corresponding descriptive statistics (such as min, max, mean, standard deviation, etc.) used as features for the classifiers would be enough to identify fraudsters.

4.3   Scenario 3: Simulation of Structuring Behavior

In the "simulation of structuring behavior" scenario, we focused on the second stage of money laundering - structuring. This stage is usually described by the fraudsters' attempts to conceal the source of their illegal income by laundering the money through multiple bank accounts and banks. This process should, ideally, hide the trail of the money and make it very hard to track the money to its original owner. If the fraudsters are using a complicated enough scheme of money flow, the investigation of money laundering becomes very cumbersome.

The normal agents, again, perform normal transactions such as paying the phone bill or paying rent. They get their income from a smaller set of 30 corporate agents. They behave responsibly - not making transactions that would put their account into a deficit while trying to make the transactions that are necessary for their everyday functioning. On the other hand, the fraudsters get some of their income from cash deposits and some from transactions from accounts in different banks. Their behavior is interesting mainly in their motivation to hide the source of income. They try to "circulate" the money around in their friend circle so as to keep the investigator confused. When the right time comes, or enough money is on their account balance, they send the money to the account that is supposed to accumulate the money. If we had a look at the graph that represents the agents and their connections, we could see that some connections to their friends are stronger than the connections of normal agents to their friends.

In this simulation, we introduced two new types of agents: small number of corporate agents simulating sending wages to normal agents and accumulating accounts accumulating circulated illegal money.

In order to be able to identify a fraudulent behavior of the agents, we need to integrate account network or graph features into our model. We use local graph features (derived from agent's direct neighbourhood such as probability and frequency of doing transactions with the agent's connections). Global graph features (account features derived from the whole graph) would be very hard or impossible to obtain in the real world scenario (due to practical and computational reasons), as it would require to process the whole network of interconnected accounts from internal systems of many different banks.

We computed the probability of making a transaction with each of the agent's friend, and from this array of probabilities, we computed the typical descriptive statistics such as quantiles or standard deviation. The same was done for the frequency of making transactions with the agent's friends.

The setup of the simulation was similar to the previous ones: 9,500 normal agents and 500 fraudsters. In this scenario, dynamic fraudster agent behavior was used to the full extent, which would be impossible if we were to use some other kind of simulation (f.e. microsimulation). The agents were given an intelligent set of rules so that they would try to cover the tracks of the money as well as behave similarly to the normal agents. The fraudsters' behavior was affected by the behavior of other agents. Instead of picking transaction amounts from a random distribution, fraudsters would decide, based on their current balance, whether they want to shuffle the money around to their friends or send the money to the accumulating account. If they decided they would shuffle the money, it was then randomly decided on how many of their friends would be receiving the money and how big the money amounts would be.

5   Evaluation

We evaluate the applicability of the proposed simulation framework in two ways:

1. We evaluate applicability of simulation scenarios by application of standard methods for fraudulent account detection on simulated data.
2. We evaluate similarity of simulated data created using statistics of small sample of real data and the original data.

5.1   Evaluation on Fraudulent Account Detection

We evaluate the applicability of the simulation framework and simulation scenarios by application of standard methods for fraudulent account detection on simulated data. We compare accuracy of multiple standard supervised methods for anomaly detection on bank transaction data.

The feature extraction process is comprised of extracting aggregated values (quartiles, min, max, mean, standard deviation, kurtosis and skew) per agent on transaction amounts, average monthly deposit, transaction frequency and probabilities of communication with connected accounts.

For our evaluation purposes we used four standard classification algorithms: Logistic Regression, Decision Tree, Random Forest and SVM. We used grid search with 10-fold cross-validation hyperparameter optimization strategy on 70% of data for each compared algorithm. The best model was then trained on this 70% of the dataset without cross-validation and evaluated on the remaining 30% of the dataset. Every evaluated metric (Precision, Recall, F1) was evaluated on the fraudster class. Results on datasets prepared for scenarios 1 to 3 are displayed on Figs. 4, 5 and 6 respectively.

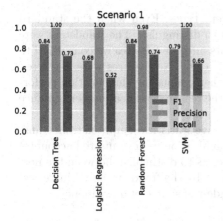

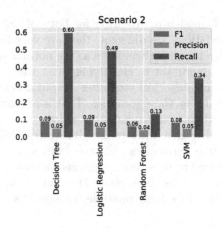

Fig. 4. Classification algorithms comparison on the hardest scenario 1 dataset.

Fig. 5. Classification algorithms comparison on the hardest scenario 2 dataset.

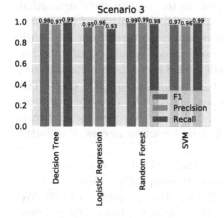

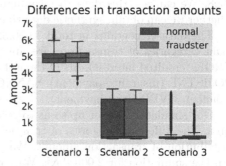

Fig. 6. Classification algorithms comparison on the dataset for scenario 3.

Fig. 7. Transaction amounts for various agent types for all scenarios.

In Fig. 4, we can clearly see that the identified features (consisting mainly of descriptive statistics computed from the transaction amount) were enough to achieve reasonably good performance on the hardest dataset. One of the main reasons why this is the case is that the normal agents were drawing samples from a Gaussian distribution and the fraudsters were using a modified lognormal distribution to draw samples from. The modification made it look more like a Gaussian distribution, but even when the means of the distributions were the same, the two distributions were not completely indistinguishable. Transaction amounts for both classes on all evaluated scenarios are displayed on Fig. 7.

A different case may be observed in Fig. 5 showing the results for scenario 2. The sampled distribution from which amounts for cash deposits were drawn was a Gaussian distribution for both of the agent types. Even when the standard deviations are different, they are very hard to distinguish. The fraudsters were able to mask themselves as the normal agents and the features we considered to be important in classifying them were insufficient. No features were extracted from categorical attributes of transactions when evaluating classification performance on these scenarios. That is probably the reason classification performance on data from scenario 2 is so low.

In Fig. 6, the local graph features (descriptive statistics computed from transaction frequencies and probabilities of communication with connected accounts) proved to provide enough classification power as to distinguish between the normal and fraudster class. This can be explained by the fraudster users' increased interest in doing multiple transactions to hide the source of dirty money.

5.2   Comparison of Simulated Data to Real Dataset

In order to demonstrate the usefulness of our simulator, we need to show that it also works for the purpose of simulating data with a small sample of real-world data used as training dataset. For the purpose of testing this data simulation case, we will be using the KDD'99 Berka dataset [4]. It consists of real world bank transaction data (from a bank in Czech republic) captured from 1993 until 1998. We can use this data to meaningfully set up our simulator and observe whether we can obtain synthetic data that will look close to the original dataset.

The dataset contains in total 1,056,320 transactions from 4,500 users. The main categories of transactions are: unspecified, DUCHOD (old-age pension), UROK (credited interest), SIPO (household), SLUZBY (payment for services), POJISTNE (insurance payment), SANKC. UROK (sanction interest if negative balance), UVER (loan payment).

Our simulator was set up so as to resemble the Berka data as much as possible. The different categories of transactions were sampled for histogram data distribution of transaction amount. We set the number of agents to 4,500. We ran the simulation for 2,000 days. We counted the probability of a transaction being from a certain category and used that to generate the transaction categories. We also computed the frequency of transactions from these categories and adjusted the probability of making the transactions accordingly. We also measured the average and median number of connections between agents and adjusted our simulation accordingly. Most of the agents in our simulation have 4 to 5 connections (to other friendly agents), while the rest will have from 1 (minimum) to 16 (maximum) connections.

In Fig. 12, we show the distributions of amount for the different transaction categories and compare them with the real data distribution. Table 1 shows that the synthetic distributions are very similar to the real distributions, using the chi-square test. We have found that there is no significant difference between these distributions. In Figs. 8, 9, 10 and 11, we show four q-q plots for transaction amounts of four different transaction categories. All of the comparisons, whether it is a histogram, a chi-square test or a q-q plot, show a very high similarity to the real distributions. This fact supports our hypothesis that we are able to

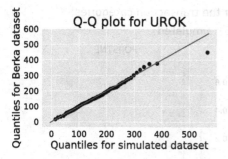

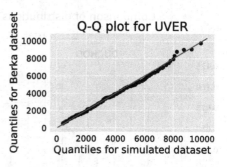

Fig. 8. Q-Q plot for UROK transaction category.

Fig. 9. Q-Q plot for UVER transaction category.

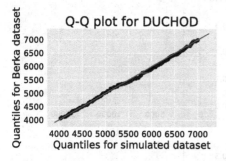

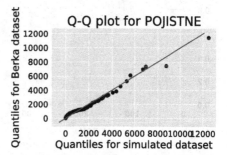

Fig. 10. Q-Q plot for DUCHOD transaction category.

Fig. 11. Q-Q plot for POJISTNE transaction category.

Table 1. Chi-square tests comparing the simulated data distributions with the real Berka dataset distributions.

Transaction category	F-statistic	P-value	Degrees of freedom
DUCHOD	0.0210	0.999	9
POJISTNE	0.0219	0.999	9
SANKC. UROK	0.0382	0.999	9
SIPO	0.0159	0.999	9
SLUZBY	0.0052	0.997	2
UROK	0.0227	0.999	9
UVER	0.0363	0.999	9
Unspecified	0.0156	0.999	9

simulate real-world looking data using our simulator (to the extent of properties and patterns intentionally inserted into the simulation), provided that we have statistical information about the dataset.

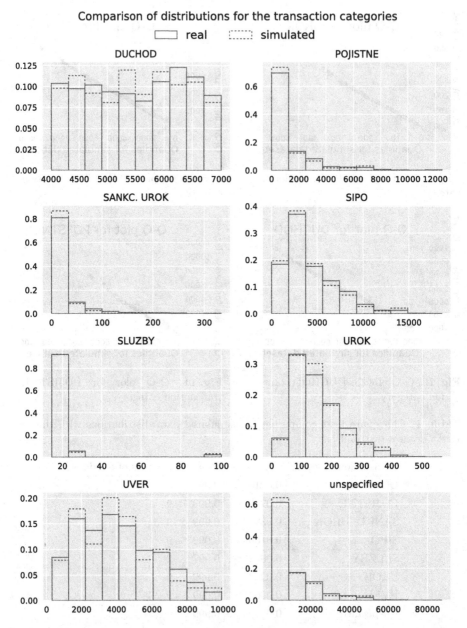

Fig. 12. Comparison of real Berka data [4] distributions (red full line) with the simulated data distributions (blue dotted line). Histograms are showing frequencies of transaction amount intervals for various transaction types (Color figure online)

6 Conclusions

We have presented an extensible multi-agent based simulation framework for transaction data generation. The usefulness of this framework was illustrated on simulating three different money laundering scenarios and it is applicable for other types of scenarios as well. We evaluated the applicability of the presented simulation framework by creating multiple money laundering scenarios and on classification of fraudster accounts from simulated transactions. We showed that aggregated features extracted from transaction data on account level could be used successfully to detect suspicious behaviour: avoiding reporting limits and simple forms of structuring. To be able to detect large amounts of cash deposit, one should use features extracted from categorical transaction attributes.

A second evaluation of our framework was done by creating a synthesized dataset by using statistical information from a real-world bank transaction dataset from the KDD '99 competition. We carefully set the simulator so that a lot of the properties of the simulator would resemble the real world dataset (f.e. number of agents, number of connections, etc.). We evaluated the transaction category distributions between the real world dataset and the synthesized dataset using histograms, chi-square tests and q-q plots. Our results show that the distributions are very similar. Therefore, this supports our hypothesis that we are able to create synthesized data that is real-world looking.

The results of classification evaluation as well as comparison to real world data presented in this paper, should be taken with caution. The purpose of the simulation and following evaluation using classification algorithms is mainly to provide insight into how simulation can be leveraged and provide support in building useful models for money laundering detection and prevention. These results in no way prove that, in order to successfully detect the specific scenarios, one such simulation is enough. The real world data are much more complex, contain many hidden patterns and have many associated sources of data not addressed in these simulation scenarios. One area where these models could provide useful insight is the analysis of specific customer segments directly modelled by the simulation. The effort to use such simulation to create real-world like looking data with all its complexities and patterns would be very hard if not impossible.

Acknowledgement. This work was partially supported by CEAI Slovakia, Scientific Grant Agency of the Slovak Republic, grants No. VG 1/0646/15 and VG 1/0667/18 and Slovak Research and Development Agency under the contract No. APVV-15-0508.

References

1. Aggarwal, C.C., Yu, P.S.: A General Survey of Privacy-Preserving Data Mining Models and Algorithms. In: Aggarwal, C.C., Yu, P.S. (eds.) Privacy-Preserving Data Mining. Advances in Database Systems, vol. 34, pp. 11–52. Springer, Boston (2008). https://doi.org/10.1007/978-0-387-70992-5_2
2. Barabási, A.L., Albert, R.: Emergence of scaling in random networks. Science **286**(439), 509–512 (1999)

3. Barse, E.L., Kvarnstrom, H., Jonsson, E.: Synthesizing test data for fraud detection systems. In: Proceedings of 19th Annual Computer Security Applications Conference, pp. 384–394. IEEE (2003)
4. Berka, P., Guide to the financial data set. PKDD 2000 discovery challenge (2000)
5. Bruch, E., Atwell, J.: Agent-based models in empirical social research. Sociol. Methods Res. **44**(2), 186–221 (2015)
6. Chrysopoulos, A., Diou, C., Symeonidis, A.L., Mitkas, P.A.: Bottom-up modeling of small-scale energy consumers for effective demand response applications. Eng. Appl. Artif. Intell. **35**, 299–315 (2014)
7. Lopez-Rojas, E.A., Axelsson, S.: BankSim: a bank payment simulation for fraud detection research. In: 26th European Modeling and Simulation Symposium, EMSS 2014, pp. 144–152 (2014)
8. Lopez-Rojas, E.A., Axelsson, S.: Money laundering detection using synthetic data. In: The 27th Annual Workshop of the Swedish Artificial Intelligence Society (SAIS), no. 071, pp. 33–40 (2012)
9. Lopez-Rojas, E.A., Axelsson, S.: Multi agent based simulation (MABS) of financial transactions for anti money laundering (AML). In: Nordic Conference on Secure IT Systems, pp. 25–32. Blekinge Institute of Technology (2012)
10. Lopez-Rojas, E.A., Gorton, D., Axelsson, S.: Using the RetSim simulator for fraud detection research. Int. J. Simul. Process Model. **10**(2), 144–155 (2015)
11. Masad, D., Kazil, J.: MESA: an agent-based modeling framework. In: 14th PYTHON in Science Conference, pp. 53–60 (2015)
12. Oldham, M.: To big wing, or not to big wing, now an answer. In: Nardin, L.G., Antunes, L. (eds.) MABS 2016. LNCS (LNAI), vol. 10399, pp. 95–110. Springer, Cham (2017). https://doi.org/10.1007/978-3-319-67477-3_5
13. Philippon, D., et al.: Exploring trade and health policies influence on dengue spread with an agent-based model. In: Nardin, L.G., Antunes, L. (eds.) MABS 2016. LNCS (LNAI), vol. 10399, pp. 111–127. Springer, Cham (2017). https://doi.org/10.1007/978-3-319-67477-3_6
14. Tomita, S., Namatame, A.: Bilateral tradings with and without strategic thinking. In: Hales, D., Edmonds, B., Norling, E., Rouchier, J. (eds.) MABS 2003. LNCS (LNAI), vol. 2927, pp. 73–88. Springer, Heidelberg (2003). https://doi.org/10.1007/978-3-540-24613-8_6

The Temporality Model Time Scheduling Approach: A Practical Application

Tahina Ralitera[✉], Denis Payet, Nathan Aky, and Rémy Courdier

Laboratoire d'Informatique et de Mathématiques,
University of Reunion Island, Saint-Denis, France
{tahina.ralitera,denis.payet,remy.courdier}@univ-reunion.fr,
nathan@smg.re

Abstract. A multi-agent based simulation aims at imitating complex phenomena or processes of the real world. For that purpose, the simulation platform has the simulated model evolve by running a virtual time and by activating agents' behaviour at each advancement of the time. This time coherence is ensured by the scheduler. The way this scheduler manages the simulated time could affect the performance of the simulation platform. However, conventional time scheduling approaches have limitations in some cases. As a solution, the temporality model approach addresses a set of criteria that conventional approaches cannot achieve. In this paper, we show the functioning of such a scheduler as well as a demonstration of the performance advantages of this type of approach.

Keywords: Scheduler approach · Temporality model ·
Multi-agent simulation

1 Introduction

A simulation model intends to imitate phenomena that occur over time in a real-world system or process. For that purpose, the simulation platform produces an evolution of the model following a virtual time. In general, this simulated time progresses much faster than real time. That allows us to quickly obtain observations on the evolution of the studied model, and thus deduce the properties of the real system that is imitated. In a simulation platform, the virtual time management is done by the scheduler. Different approaches are used for that: the time-stepped, the event-driven and the mixed approaches (see Sect. 2). We are interested in applications for personal computers and however, these conventional time management approaches still have disadvantages in some situations as described in Sect. 2. That can affect the performances of the simulation platform. The Temporality Model approach [9] was proposed to address a number of criteria that conventional approaches cannot meet. We implemented and experimented this approach through a simulation model called the SKUADCityModel.

Supported by the Région Réunion, the L'Oréal-UNESCO for women in science fellowship and the town of Saint-Denis.

© Springer Nature Switzerland AG 2019
P. Davidsson and H. Verhagen (Eds.): MABS 2018, LNAI 11463, pp. 115–125, 2019.
https://doi.org/10.1007/978-3-030-22270-3_9

In this article, following our experiments, we show the performance advantages of this type of scheduler approach. For that purpose, we perform a comparison of performance between a version of the SKUADCityModel using the temporality model scheduling approach and another version using the time-stepped scheduling approach.

In the next section, we will describe the three classic scheduling approaches that are commonly used in agent simulators: the times-stepped approach, the event-driven approach and the mixed approach. We will show that they all have disadvantages in some situations. Then we will describe, in a general way, the temporality model approach.

2   Related Work

Classic time scheduling approaches can be classified in three categories: the time-stepped approach, the event-driven approach and the mixed approach. This section presents each one and shows a graphic representation of each corresponding simulated time axis.

2.1   The Time-Stepped Approach

The time-stepped approach is the most used approach in multi-agent systems because of the simplicity of its implementation. In this approach, the scheduler advances the simulation time by incrementing its value by a fixed duration Δt called time-step [2]. The simulated time can be represented by an axis discretized by fixed intervals (Fig. 1). For each time-step, all the simulation activities (agent cycle and possibly objects simulation) are completed before advancing to the next step. This approach is usually easier to set up. Also, it is convenient to one specific model composed of homogeneous agents that have the same activation frequency. However, the author of [6] concludes that using of a regular discretization of time is unsatisfactory when the simulated model requires taking into account actions that have highly heterogeneous frequencies. Indeed, because of their different nature, the agents could have different needs in term of activation frequency. Consequently, imposing a single frequency on all agents will be inappropriate.

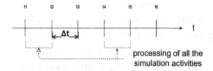

Fig. 1. Time axis for time-stepped approaches.

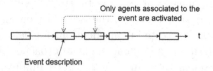

Fig. 2. Time axis for event-driven approaches.

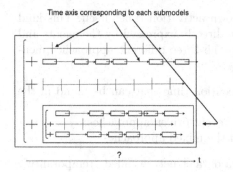

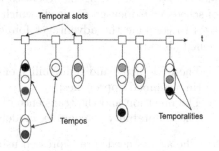

Fig. 3. Time axis for mixed approaches.

Fig. 4. Time axis for the temporality model approach.

2.2 The Event-Driven Approach

In this approach, the time axis of the simulation is continuous but the state of the system changes discretely at precise times called events. An event can be defined as the description of the agents' behaviour activation condition at a specific time. Its release date can be calculated depending on the nature of these conditions. Thus, the simulation consists in executing an orderly list of events. The time axis can be represented by a chained event list, which punctuates the axis with points that are not equitably spaced (Fig. 2).

In this approach, an agent is activated when it needs to be activated. Consequently, it is suitable in the case of highly heterogeneous agents, and thus addresses the limitation of the time-stepped approach. However, it is impossible for the user of the platform to have any control over the simulated time. Also, simulated time can take very complex forms [3]. Consequently, the calculations made by the simulator can become rather substantial.

2.3 The Mixed Approach

Mixed approaches propose to split the simulated model into sub-models. Examples can be found in [5] and [7]. To each sub-model is associated the most appropriate type of scheduler. The resulting system corresponds to the combination of the different schedulers chosen. There is therefore no global time axis (Fig. 3).

This lack of global vision causes problems if we want to make an analysis of the simulation time. Moreover, any attempt to influence the simulated time structure in order to reduce the execution time of the simulation is also prohibited [9].

2.4 The Temporality Model Approach

In multi-agent systems, an agent typically has some autonomy over the characterization of its state and its behaviour. In the same way, in the temporality model approach, the agent describes its own activation times itself. This kind of scheduler is focused on needs which are directly expressed by the agents and tries to combine the advantages found in the three different approaches mentioned above:

- The periodicity and reducibility of execution time that can be found in the time-stepped approaches;
- The precision and the transience of the event-driven approaches;
- The adaptability to complex models of the mixed approaches.

The agents needs are expressed using a data structure called "temporality".

A temporality t specifies a point on the time axis for which an agent wants to be activated. t can be defined by the tuple [9]:

$$t = \{id, d, f, p, v\} \tag{1}$$

where:

- id is the identifier of the temporality. It is used by agents to associate a specific behaviour with the temporality.
- $[d, f]$ is the time interval during which the temporality can be triggered.
- p is the time period, meaning the time interval between two executions of this temporality ($p = 0$ if the action is only executed once).
- v is the variability. It defines the accuracy below which the temporal occurrence remains valid.

A temporality activates the agent's behaviour at each time equal to $x = d + p * k$, where k is an integer such as $0 \leq k \leq n$ and n is the biggest integer that verifies $(d + p * n) = f$.

The agents define their temporalities during the simulation initialization. Afterwards, if they need to adjust their behaviour, they will be able to redefine temporalities or create new ones at any time. The scheduler immediately processes the creations and modifications, then updates the time axis.

Another particularity of the temporality model approach is the ability to add time constraints. This addresses the limitation of the event-scheduling and mixed approaches because it allows the users to influence the simulated time structure. This particularity could be important in some cases. Indeed, depending on the complexity of the simulated model, the user can be forced to reduce the simulation execution time. That could be done by constraining the simulation platform and could lead to even a loss of result precision. However, it is better than not getting any results at all. The event-driven approach does not allow that.

This is done by specifying two regulation properties:

- The minimum time-step Δt_{min} that indicates that two distinct activation dates should be separated by a duration at least equal to the value of Δt_{min}. If such a situation occurs during the analysis of the temporalities, the scheduler will use the variability parameter v of each of the temporalities to determine if they should be separated from each other or regrouped together on the same date.

- The default time period value that is used for some agents that do not define any temporalities during the initialization of the simulation.

As seen in Fig. 4, the scheduler processes the temporalities using two structures of data:

- The Temporal/Time slot is a point on the time axis where the scheduler will activate the agent's behaviour.
- The tempo is a structure that group all the temporalities which are located on the same time slot and which have the same time period. This time period characterizes the tempo. It means that all the temporalities it contains have the same activation rhythm. The scheduler advances the simulated time by successively making it take the positions indicated by the time slots. In each time slot, all the tempos are processed. It produces the execution of all the behaviours associated with the temporalities they contain.

Thus, Payet et al. [9] list different benefits of the Temporality Model compared to classical approaches.

- According to Helleboogh et al. [4] the time management system should be able to adapt to the specificities of the model to be simulated. This criterion is not met in time-stepped approaches while by definition, the Temporality Model is mainly based on that.
- Because of the regulation properties: the minimum time step, the default period and the temporal variability attribute, the Temporality Model allows us to take into account the constraints that the user wishes to impose on the simulator. The event-driven and mixed approaches do not allow that.
- In this approach, the time management is homogeneous. It is flexible enough to easily adapt to time-stepped simulation and to pure event-driven simulation without changing the nature of the simulated time building support. Indeed, in the extreme cases, if no agent defines any temporality, it automatically fall sback into a time-stepped approach and if all the agents are complex and express a large number of temporalities, it ends up with an event-driven type of scheduling.
- The approach handles a cumulative characterization of time. Indeed, this approach has the activities as granularity. Consequently, the behavior of complex agents can be written by different people specialized in a particular type of activity.
- It handles an incremental complexity and minimizes the impact on execution performance. It means that compared to other approaches, the cost is closer of the time-stepped approaches.

In their paper, Payet et al. [9] demonstrated these benefits with assumptions and a theoretical comparison between the different classical approaches and the temporality model. In this article, we support this demonstration with practical applications.

3 Case Study

The proposed case study is about agent-based simulation of individual electric transport. The chosen territory is the city of Saint-Denis, capital of Reunion Island. It is a French island in the Indian Ocean with an area of $142.79\,\text{km}^2$ and which is composed of 146,985 inhabitants in 2015.

3.1 The Agent Model

In this simulation model, the agents are plug-in electric vehicle (PEV) owners. They make travel decisions according to their perception and their memories. The model uses the activity-based approach. That means that the agents move from one place to another following an activity schedule. Consequently, the travels result from demands for personal activities (work, shopping, leisure, going home) that the individuals need or wish to perform. The agents are also capable of adapting their behaviour, given a particular situation such as low battery charge.

Their goal is to conduct all their activities using its electric vehicle and the charging stations at their disposal. As a resource, they owns an electric vehicle with an average power consumption and a charge capacity. The activity profile AP_i for each group i of PEV owners is defined with a list of 4-tuples [1]:

$$AP_i = (ACT_j, MDT_j, SD_j, PD_j) \qquad (2)$$

Where ACT_j represents the activity j, MDT_j the mean departure time, SD_j the standard deviation, and PD_j the probability of departure for the activity j.

3.2 The Environment Modeling Elements

The agents' environment is represented by a collection of entities corresponding to fragments of the physical environment. It is defined using Geographic Information System (GIS). It is composed of the superposition of layers:

- The building layer is composed of polygons that represent administrative boundaries,
- The road layer is composed of polylines that represent the road network,
- The area of interest layer is composed of polygons or points that represent the location of residential, working, commercial and leisure areas.

The shape files and statistical data are taken as input of the simulation model. They are used at different levels such as for environment modeling, for the calculation of the population distribution or the PEV consumption. In our case, the agents are moving over 10,215 portions of roads and in a $142.8\,\text{km}^2$ of territory.

The following section describe the SKUADCityModel which is an implementation this simulation model built upon the SimSKUAD simulation platform.

4   The SKUADCityModel

4.1   SKUAD

SKUAD stands for "Software Kit for Ubiquitous Agent Development". This free, multi-platform toolkit allows us to create ambient and ubiquitous multi-agent systems.

Ambient multi-agent systems means that agents can operate in our real environment. Ubiquitous means that they operate in our real environment regardless of the physical substrate on which they are running. Thus, SKUAD can run on different devices which have microprocessors such as classic computers or Raspberry Pi. It also runs on a specific version on micro-controller chips such as Arduino Chips or ESP8266.

This toolbox has been developed since 2013 by the Collective Adaptive Systems Research Group in the laboratory of Mathematics and Computer Science (LIM) at the University of Reunion Island. The idea comes from the observation of the outburst of the Internet of Things, and the necessity to have a software that can make this mass of objects more consistent.

SKUAD is composed of four software blocks organized as shown in Fig. 5.

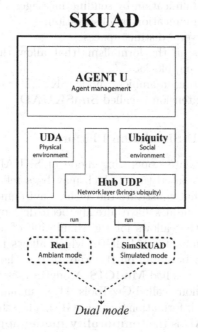

Fig. 5. Diagram of SKUAD architecture

1. HubUDP is the network part of the toolkit. It is responsible for making all the parts above communicate, even if multiple instances are executed on different devices. It is a zeroconf middleware and allows for the creation of overlay network.

2. UDA is a software architecture that is responsible for the normalization of the communication between any device (actuators, sensors or whatever) and a software code, through an introspective process. With these mechanisms, it is possible to link agents to our real environment (through different devices).
3. Ubiquity operates for social interactions. Indeed, to match the definition of multi-agent systems, SKUAD must be able to handle another form of interaction. Ubiquity allows interaction (explicit and implicit communication) between agents.

The ability of an agent to interact is specified by slots that can have two natures:

- The physical slots that characterize the physical interaction abilities of an agent. For example its ability to perform actions or readings on hardware devices.
- The social slots of space that characterize the social interaction abilities of an agent. For example its ability to make implicit or explicit communication with other agents.

    The social interaction area of agents is called "space". In SKUAD, two agents can interact if they are within the same space. There could be two possible kinds of communications:

    • Explicit communication by sending messages;
    • Implicit communication by observation.

    There may be several distinct spaces.
4. AgentU encompasses all the formalisms that allow the creation of agents, based on the underlying blocks.

    In addition to operating in ambient mode, SKUAD can also be used in simulated mode. This extension is called **SimSKUAD**.

4.2   The SimSKUAD Simulation Platform

SimSKUAD is the simulated operating mode of SKUAD. In this mode, the agents operate on a simulated time (which may be a reflection of the physical time) and the devices that constitute the agents environment are virtual.

Different optional modules have already been developed for SimSKUAD. Examples are Mod2D that allows for the simulating of agents to be executed in a continuous environment or ModGrid which allows to simulate a discrete space. More details can be found on the website [8]. The module in which we will focus in this paper is called **ModGIS**. ModGIS uses the same open-source library as Repast Simphony called GeoTools [11] to manage the display and for the use of Geographical Information System (GIS). The scheduler approach used by default in SimSKUAD is the **temporality model approach**.

4.3   The SKUADCityModel

The SKUADCityModel is built upon the ModGIS module of the SimSKUAD simulation platform. It uses Java language. The time scheduler approach used by default in this simulation model is the temporality model approach. However, its architecture is flexible enough to allow us to easily modify or replace the scheduler. Thus, we were also able to run the SKUADCityModel using the time-stepped approach.

5   Confrontation of the Different Approaches

One of our objective, when using the Temporality Model approach, is to minimize the cost in term of execution performance. As said earlier, the goal is to have an execution performance that are the closest of the time-stepped approach. In this section, we will illustrate the performance advantages of the temporality model approach by comparing it with the results we got when we used the time-stepped approach. For that purpose we vary the number of agents. Then, we made a comparison of the results based on two criteria:

- The execution duration performance: to show that the results are quite close.
- The scalability: to show how the simulation model can scale up depending on the used time scheduler approach.

The simulation is composed of a total of 81,602 agents, 10,215 portions of roads and 142.8 km^2 of territory. We simulated 24 h of activities. The configuration of the used computer, for these experiments, is as follow: core i7, 8 gigabytes of RAM and a solid state drive. Figure 6 shows the results of the first experiments we carried.

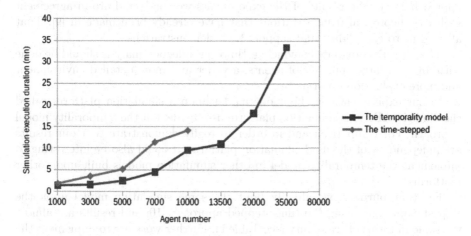

Fig. 6. Experiments results

The results clearly show that in case where the time-stepped approach is used, the maximum number of agents that could be supported by the simulation platform does not exceed 10,000 while the use of temporality model approach enables us to simulate almost 35,000 agents. In addition to this gain, in the case of the use of the temporality model approach, the results, in terms of execution duration performance, are quite acceptable not only because they are getting closer, or in some cases are even better than the results we obtained using the time-stepped approach, but also they are very reasonable compared to the 24 simulated hours.

These results are in line with the demonstrations made in [9]. That shows the performance advantages of this Temporality Model approach. Especially, it allows the simulation to scale while maintaining acceptable performance.

6   Conclusion and Further Work

Agents scheduling management is a critical process in simulation platforms. Unfortunately, most conventional scheduling approaches all have disadvantages that are too restrictive in certain situations. Payet et al. [9] proposes the temporality model approach as a potential solution that fulfil most of the requirements that a scheduler should meet in the case of multi-agent simulation platforms. This approach is intended to combine the main principles that are advantageous in classical approaches. That has been demonstrated by illustrative examples based on theoretical assumptions. In this paper, we fill this demonstration with practical results. For that purpose, we made a performance comparison between two implementations based on the same simulation model, but using two different scheduling approaches: the time-stepped approach and the temporality model approach. We showed how our simulation can scale while maintaining acceptable execution duration performance depending on the time scheduling approach used. The results of the experiments we conducted are in agreement with the theoretical demonstrations that have already been made in [9]. That allowed us to consolidate and support their demonstrations.

These results are quite convincing. However a deeper analysis should be done with an even larger number of agents, a wider and more detailed environment and more evaluation criteria.

In our experiments, we built our model upon a simulation platform called the SimSKUAD. This simulation platform uses by default the temporality model approach. For comparison and in order to really demonstrate that our results are independent of the used simulation platform, it could also be interesting to implement the temporality model in other simulation models built upon other platforms.

For that purpose, we already built the same simulation model upon the Repast Simphony using the time-stepped approach [10] and results are almost the same in terms of scalability (see Table 1). Further work are to implement the temporality model approach in Repast Simphony and to compare the results with those described in this paper.

In this paper, we are interested in application on classic personal computers. That means we do not consider the cases of multiprocessing hardware environments or distributed and parallel simulation execution. These tracks could be also interesting to explore.

Table 1. Simulation execution duration, experiments on a simulation model built upon the Repast Simphony simulation platform and using the time-stepped approach

Time step (mn)	1000 agents	5000 agents	7000 agents	10000 agents
20	5.21	28.66	37.55	Out of memory
15	4.64	34.05	145.6	Out of memory
10	3.56	159.38	Out of memory	Out of memory
5	2.48	Out of memory	Out of memory	Out of memory
1	2.06	Out of memory	Out of memory	Out of memory

References

1. Bustos-Turu, G., Dam, K.H.V., Acha, S., Shah, N.: Estimating plug-in electric vehicle demand flexibility through an agent-based simulation model. In: 2014 IEEE PES Innovative Smart Grid Technologies Conference Europe (ISGT-Europe), pp. 1–6. IEEE (2014)
2. Fujimoto, R.M.: Time management in the high level architecture. Simulation **71**(6), 388–400 (1998). https://doi.org/10.1177/003754979807100604
3. Galler, H.P.: Discrete-time and continuous-time approaches to dynamic microsimulation reconsidered. National Centre for Social and Economic Modelling (1997)
4. Helleboogh, A., Holvoet, T., Weyns, D., Berbers, Y.: Extending time management support for multi-agent systems. In: Davidsson, P., Logan, B., Takadama, K. (eds.) MABS 2004. LNCS (LNAI), vol. 3415, pp. 37–48. Springer, Heidelberg (2005). https://doi.org/10.1007/978-3-540-32243-6_4
5. Luke, S., Cioffi-Revilla, C., Panait, L., Sullivan, K.: MASON: a new multi-agent simulation toolkit. In: Proceedings of the 2004 Swarmfest Workshop, Michigan, USA, vol. 8, pp. 316–327 (2004)
6. Michel, F.: Formalisme, outils et éléments méthodologiques pour la modélisation et la simulation multi-agents. (Formalism, tools and methodological elements for the modeling and simulation of multi-agents systems). Ph.D. thesis, Montpellier 2 University, France (2004). https://tel.archives-ouvertes.fr/tel-01610063
7. Minar, N., Burkhart, R., Langton, C., Askenazi, M., et al.: The swarm simulation system: a toolkit for building multi-agent simulations (1996)
8. Payet, D.: Official website of skuad (2018). http://skuad.onover.top/. Accessed 15 Jul 2018
9. Payet, D., Courdier, R., Ralambondrainy, T., Sébastien, N.: Le modèle à temporalité: pour un équilibre entre adéquation et optimisation du temps dans les simulations agent. In: Systemes Multi-Agents, Articulation entre l'individuel et le collectif - JFSMA 2006 - Quatorzieme journees francophones sur les systemes multi-agents, Annecy, France, 18–20 October 2006, pp. 63–76 (2006)
10. Ralitera, T., Ferard, M., Bustos-Turu, G., van Dam, K.H., Courdier, R.: Steps towards simulating smart cities and smart islands with a shared generic framework - a case study of London and Reunion Island. In: SMARTGREENS 2017 - Proceedings of the 6th International Conference on Smart Cities and Green ICT Systems, Porto, Portugal, 22–24 April 2017, pp. 329–336 (2017)
11. Turton, I.: Open Source Approaches in Spatial Data Handling. Springer, Heidelberg (2008)

Multi-agent Systems Society for Power and Energy Systems Simulation

Gabriel Santos[1], Tiago Pinto[1,2(✉)], and Zita Vale[3]

[1] GECAD – Research Group on Intelligent Engineering and Computing for
Advanced Innovation and Development, Institute of Engineering,
Polytechnic of Porto (ISEP/IPP), Porto, Portugal
{gajls,tcp}@isep.ipp.pt
[2] BISITE Research Group – University of Salamanca, Salamanca, Spain
tpinto@usal.es
[3] Polytechnic of Porto (ISEP/IPP), Porto, Portugal
zav@isep.ipp.pt

Abstract. A key challenge in the power and energy field is the development of decision-support systems that enable studying big problems as a whole. The interoperability between multi-agent systems that address specific parts of the global problem is essential. Ontologies ease the interoperability between heterogeneous systems providing semantic meaning to the information exchanged between the various parties. The use of ontologies within Smart Grids has been proposed based on the Common Information Model, which defines a common vocabulary describing the basic components used in electricity transportation and distribution. However, these ontologies are focused on utilities' needs. The development of ontologies that allow the representation of diverse knowledge sources is essential, aiming at supporting the interaction between entities of different natures, facilitating the interoperability between these systems. This paper proposes a set of ontologies to enable the interoperability between different types of agent-based simulators, namely regarding electricity markets, the smart grid, and residential energy management. A case study based on real data shows the advantages of the proposed approach in enabling comprehensive power system simulation studies.

Keywords: Multi-agent simulation · Power and energy systems ·
Semantic interoperability

1 Introduction

The emergence of liberalized electricity markets (EM) completely revolutionized the power sector business. Several challenges have been brought by the sector's restructuring process. It required the transformation of the conceptual models that previously dominated the power sector [1].

This work has received funding from the European Union's Horizon 2020 research and innovation programme under the Marie Sklodowska-Curie grant agreement No. 641794 (project DREAM-GO) and grant agreement No. 703689 (project ADAPT). This work has also been supported by National funds by FCT in the scope of Gabriel Santos PhD (SFRH/BD/118487/2016).

© Springer Nature Switzerland AG 2019
P. Davidsson and H. Verhagen (Eds.): MABS 2018, LNAI 11463, pp. 126–137, 2019.
https://doi.org/10.1007/978-3-030-22270-3_10

The market became more competitive, but also more complex, posing new challenges to its participants, forcing them to rethink their market strategies and consequently their behaviour. The new challenges that EM restructuring produced increased the importance of EM operation study. The raised complexity and competitiveness of the market together with its unpredictable evolution, hardens the decision-making process [2].

Several models have emerged trying to overcome market challenges. Despite the guidance provided by some pioneer countries experience in what regards the implemented market models' performance, it is still premature to take definitive conclusions. Thereby, the use of tools that allow the study of different market mechanisms and the relationships between market entities becomes essential. The use of simulation tools becomes decisive in order to study, analyse, and test different alternatives for markets' structure and evolution, providing entities with decision support tools to address the new challenges. These tools aim to handle with EM constant evolving reality, ensuring the appropriate solutions to actors adapt themselves to this new reality, acquiring experience to operate in this changing economic, financial, and regulatory environment. Operators must guarantee a transparent and competitive market while market players try to minimize their costs and maximize their profits [3].

For the analysis of dynamic and complex environments, such as the EM, multi-agent based simulators are particularly well suited [4]. Multi-agent approaches enable an easy inclusion of: new market models and mechanisms, new types of market players and interactions [4]. Some reference modelling tools of this domain are: the Agent-based Modelling of Electricity Systems (AMES) [5]; the Electricity Market Complex Adaptive System (EMCAS) [6], the Multi-Agent Simulator of Competitive Electricity Markets (MASCEM) [7] and Multi-Agent Smart Grid simulation Platform (MASGriP) [8] developed by the authors research team.

These are relevant tools but are often directed to the perspective of market operators and regulators, while not providing an adequate decision support to the participating players. In this scope, AiD-EM (Adaptive Decision Support for Electricity Market Negotiations) has been developed [9] with the objective of aiding players in their negotiation process.

The adequate applicability of multi-agent simulation to the study of EM has already been confirmed. However, there is a lack of interoperability between the various systems. These tools focus only on the study of the different market players and mechanisms, and on the analysis of the relations between those entities, but they still do not allow interoperability with heterogeneous tools of the same domain. These systems can benefit significantly from sharing their models with each other, allowing agent-based players from external systems to participate in the same market environment, from which they can learn from each other. Such interoperability would allow a strong improvement in EM studies and development EM simulators must be flexible in order to handle this complex and evolving reality, providing players with proper tools to adapt themselves to this dynamic reality and learn from experience. This is discussed in [10], where a short motivation for the need of developing ontologies as a way to enable the interoperability among heterogeneous multi-agent systems is addressed, culminating on the discussion on the expected advantages of creating a so-called Multi-Agent Systems Society, in which different systems interact with each other using the ontologies as communication language, and also enabling the interaction with other external systems that may arise in the future.

This paper provides a step forward in this domain, by introducing a set of ontologies, including the *Electricity Markets Ontology* (EMO) and specific ontologies for the power and energy systems' domain, designed to provide the means to achieve interoperability between power and energy multi-agent simulation platforms. Using these ontologies, a society of multi-agent systems is designed and developed. This MAS society allows integrating the various MAS, which enables the simulation of scenarios involving entities from the final consumer, through the management of resources by aggregators, to participants and operators of wholesale EM. In this way it is possible to undertake joint simulations between the various systems, allowing a more comprehensive study; and to enable the joint management of multiple knowledge sources from different natures, by integrating the systems with the several sources of data, through a common language.

After this introductory section, an overview of the proposed MAS society is provided in Sect. 2. Section 3 presents the proposed ontologies, while Sect. 4 features a case study based on real data from several European EM operators. Finally, the conclusions are presented in Sect. 5.

2 Multi-agent Systems Society

Power and energy systems are complex and dynamic environments, characterized by constant changes. Studying such complex systems requires complex modelling and simulation tools, to enable capturing the complete reality. For this purpose, this work proposes an agent architecture that is composed by multiple independent MAS, directed to the study of specific parts of the system, which, through the interaction of the involved agents, enable modelling the system as a whole.

The different MAS that compose the MAS society are developed in JAVA language and use the JADE platform to implement the agents, making the whole system FIPA (Foundation for Intelligent Physical Agents) compliant. In addition, to achieve interoperability between systems, the different MAS use ontologies that allow the sharing of vocabulary and mapping of concepts between systems, so that they can communicate. The ontologies are formulated in OWL DL, with representation in RDF/XML and are presented in Sect. 3. In order to allow the interoperability between the systems, ontologies enable them to speak the same language and to understand the same concepts and terms, preventing different interpretations of the same information. Two types of ontologies are used. The first type is conceptual ontologies, which are the basis for communication between systems. These ontologies allow the description of the vocabulary that is shared between the systems. The second type of ontology is related to the procedural part of the systems (application ontology), and it is used to describe the way the systems work through the description of its services and communications, detailing inputs and outputs.

The MAS society includes several independent MAS, which cover the entire energy system, from the simulation from wholesale electricity markets until the environment inside consumers' houses. The electricity market simulation is performed by

MASCEM [4]. MASCEM accommodates the simulation of a diversity of market models through a multi-agent model that includes agents to represent the market operator, the system operator, buyers, sellers and aggregators. MASCEM also enables the participation of external agents in market simulations, such as small players that are part of other systems, e.g. Smart Grid (SG) operators or other aggregators.

The decision support to market negotiations is provided by another MAS, AiD-EM [9]. AiD-EM includes agents to perform several tasks, such as the optimization of markets participation portfolio, and the decision support in auction based markets and in bilateral contracts.

The modelling of smaller players at the microgrid and SG level is provided by MASGriP, which simulates, manages and controls the most relevant players acting in a SG environment [8]. This system includes fully simulated players, which interact with software agents that control real hardware. This enables the development of a complex system capable of performing simulations with an agent society that contains both real infrastructures and simulated players, providing the means to test alternative approaches (Energy Resource Management (ERM) algorithms, Demand Response (DR), negotiation procedures, among others) in a realistic simulation setting [11].

The Intelligent Decision Support (IDeS) MAS provides several services to external systems, namely: forecast algorithms (i.e. artificial neural networks, SVM and fuzzy inference systems) to be used to forecast consumption, generation, market prices, etc; DR programs; ERM systems for SG and microgrid levels, among others. SCADA House Intelligent Management (SHIM) is a building energy management system, whose main goal is testing, simulating, and validating new algorithms and methodologies to apply in house/buildings' management [14]. In order to obtain a realistic simulation, the platform comprises real equipment such as several types of loads, mini and micro distributed generation (photovoltaic panels, wind generator), and storage systems that allow the simulation of the electric vehicles behaviour.

To ensure the simulation of complex scenarios, SHIM is able to control real loads and virtual loads simulating the characteristics of the real ones. The system is composed of different modules that are grouped into three different parts: the Data acquisition, the Actuators, and the Intelligent Applications where is included the learning algorithms. The detailed information of the structure can be found in [12]. The control of physical devices is accomplished by the connection to another MAS, the PLCMAS. The PLCMAS allows to test the scenarios in a real environment, being able to apply the results to physical devices, making them act accordingly. These devices are essentially lights, sockets and HVAC, and need to be connected to a Programmable Logic Controller (PLC).

Finally, an innovative tool is also used for the control and simulation of the MAS society. The Tools Control Centre (TOOCC) allows the simulation of the various systems/algorithms independently, as well as the joint simulation of some or all systems present in the agent society. TOOCC also facilitates the automatic analysis of the various simulations and knowledge sources, in an integrated manner [13].

The main advantage of the proposed MAS society is to enable the study and simulation of diverse and complex scenarios involving one or more systems devoted to distinct problems. Therefore, different complex dynamics between the agents of the different MAS can be accomplished and personalized, configured and analysed using

TOOCC. The proposed MAS society enables modelling the power and energy system as a whole, by representing the most relevant players through software agents, in the respective specific MAS.

3 Ontologies for MAS Interoperability

Currently, MAS in the power system's domain are developed with their own specific ontologies. These systems share common concepts that are differently represented between the independently developed ontologies, and translating these concepts automatically is not straightforward. In order to take full advantage of the functionalities of those systems, there is a growing need for knowledge exchange between them.

This paper proposes the use of ontologies for the interoperability of multi-agent simulation platforms in the power and energy domain, which can be extended in a way to enable the full interoperability between those systems. The ontologies provide the means to successfully exchange meaningful information that can be easily interpreted by software agents. On the other hand, using a reasoner, ontologies also enable to infer knowledge from the gathered information. Ontologies are used to enable semantic interoperability between heterogeneous agents and/or agent-based platforms.

3.1 EMO Specification

The EMO incorporates abstract concepts and axioms referring to the main existing EM. This ontology aims to be as inclusive as possible so that it can be extended and reused in the development of (lower level) market-specific ontologies. It was kept as simple as possible in order to facilitate its reuse and extension independently of the market's features and/or rules. However, given that the suggested ontologies were developed considering its use by agent based simulation tools, some markets' constraints were also defined in EMO. Figure 1 illustrates EMO's relations between the identified classes and object and data properties. From Fig. 1 it is possible to see the object properties represented in blue and the data properties defined within each class with the respective data types. The orange relations represent the inferred object properties, which are inverse properties of the ones defined in blue in the opposite direction.

EMO has expressivity *ALCHIQ(D)*. The *AL* (*Attributive Language*) is the base language allowing: (i) atomic negation, *i.e.* the negation of concept names that do not appear on the left side of axioms; (ii) concept intersection; (iii) universal restrictions; and (iv) limited existential quantification. *C* is the *Complex concept negation* extension. The *H* extension is related with the *role Hierarchy* (e.g. the sub properties). The *I* extension represents the *Inverse properties*. The *Q* extension are the *Qualified cardinality restrictions*, *i.e.* cardinality restrictions with fillers other than ⊤. And finally, the *(D)* refers to the use of datatype properties, data values or data types.

The definition of an **Area** includes a string *name*, a double *minPrice* and a double *maxPrice*. All the three data properties are defined as *Functional*. A functional property is a property that only relates the same subject to one single object/value. Each EM area

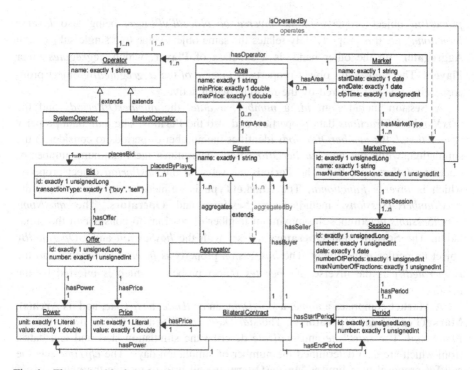

Fig. 1. *Electricity Markets Ontology* (EMO) (Available online: http://www.mascem.gecad.isep. ipp.pt/ontologies/imgs/fig2.png)

has an identifying name and its minimum and maximum prices are usually defined in its market rules.

An **Operator** includes only a *name*, while the **MarketOperator** and **SystemOperator** classes are extended from **Operator**. Other types of operators may be present in different EM, which can be defined is each market's ontology after importing the EMO.

A **Period** is here identified only with an *id* and (period) *number*. These two properties are both *Functional* as well, and it has been found important to include them in this ontology due to simulation and data storage purposes. It is certain that a period (of time) can also be defined with a start and end instants, but that terminology was left open so that, if required, one can always extend its definition in the ontology by importing EMO. Both **Price** and **Power** are defined as a set of a *unit* (e.g. EUR and MW respectively) and a *value* in double, being these two data properties *Functional* as well. An **Offer**, in turn, includes an *id*, a *number* and exactly a **Power** and a **Price** set by the object properties *hasPower* and *hasPrice* respectively. These two object properties are also *Functional*.

A **Bid** also includes an *id*, in addition to a *transactionType* ("*buy*" and "*sell*" only), a single **Player** (set with the *Functional* object property *placedByPlayer*) and **Offer**s (set by the *hasOffer* object property). A **Player** includes a *name*, and identifies its **Area** and placed **Bid**s with the respective object properties *fromArea* and *placesBid*. The *placesBid* object property is the *inverse of placedByPlayer*, being also *Inverse Functional, i.e.* this property only relates the same object/value to a single subject. An **Aggregator**, on the other hand, is a subclass of **Player**, which *aggregates* other **Player**s. The *aggregates* object property is *inverse of* the *aggregatedBy* object property, being this last inferred by the reasoner when active.

A **Session** includes an *id*, a *number*, a *date*, the *numberOfPeriods* and the *maxNumberOfFractions* data properties, and also the **Period**s. The *date* data property is *Functional*, the *numberOfPeriods* identifies the number of periods to consider in the simulation, while the *maxNumberOfFractions* determines the maximum number of fractions (**Offer**s) per **Bid**. The **Period**s are set with the *hasPeriod* object property, which is *Inverse Functional*. The **MarketType** is defined by an *id*, a *name*, the *maxNumberOfSessions*, including its **Session**s and **Operator**s. The *maxNumberOfSessions* determines the maximum number of sessions to consider in the simulation. The **Session**s and **Operator**s are set with the *hasSession* and *isOperatedBy* object properties respectively. The *hasSession* property is *Inverse Functional* and the *isOperatedBy* is the inverse of *operates* object property, which is inferred by the reasoner.

A **Market** comprises a *name*, a *startDate*, an *endDate*, a *cfpTime*, and its **Area**(s), **MarketType**(s) and **Operator**(s). The *startDate*, *endDate* and *cfpTime* properties are *Functional*. The *startDate* and *endDate* describe the simulation start and end dates, from which are also determined the number of simulation days. The *cfpTime* sets the call for proposal time limit a **MarketOperator** will wait to receive the players' proposals. The **Area**(s) are set through the *hasArea* property, the **MarketType**(s) by the *hasMarketType* property and the **Operator**(s) via the *hasOperator* object property.

A **BilateralContract** includes a buyer and a seller **Player**, a start and an end **Period**, a **Power** amount and a **Price** offer. The players are set by the *hasBuyer* and *hasSeller Functional* object properties. The start and end periods by the *hasStartPeriod* and *hasEndPeriod* properties respectively, where both are also *Functional*. And the *hasPower* and *hasPrice* properties set the **Power** and **Price** respectively.

Finally, the **Area**, the **Operator**, the **Period**, the **Power**, the **Price**, the **Offer**, the **Player**, the **Bid**, the **Session**, the **Market**, the **MarketType** and the **BilateralContract** classes are all *Disjoint Classes*, meaning that none of these classes has members in common. In other words, an element cannot be an instance of more than one of these classes, or else it makes the ontology inconsistent.

EMO was formulated in OWL DL, using Protégé[1] tool, and its representation is in RDF/XML. It is publicly available[2] so it can be used by third-party developers who wish to integrate their agent-based simulators with MASCEM, taking advantage of its simulation capabilities and market models. On the other hand, EMO may also be reused and extended for the development of new multi-agent simulation.

---

[1] http://protege.stanford.edu/.

[2] http://www.mascem.gecad.isep.ipp.pt/ontologies/electricity-markets.owl.

3.2   Additional Modules

To enable semantic communication between the market operator and player agents, two additional modules have been developed separately from EMO. These are: (i) the *Call For Proposal Ontology* (CFP) and (ii) the *Electricity Markets Results Ontology* (EMR). Although these are not detailed in this paper, are also publicly available[3].

The CFP has the purpose of being used by the market operator agents to ask player agents for bids to be placed in the market, and for players to send their proposals to the respective market operators. In turn, the EMR is the ontology used by market operator agents to inform player agents about their results and outcomes in the market.

Both modules have expressivity *ALCHIQ(D)*, similarly to EMO, and have also been formulated in OWL DL, being represented in RDF/XML as well.

3.3   Complementary Ontologies

The electricity market ontologies are complemented by a large number of other ontologies that are useful not only for communication purposes, but also for knowledge representation and sharing among the software agents. These ontologies can be summarized as follows:

- SEAS-ActorOntology: The SEAS Actor Ontology for the ITEA2 SEAS project
- SEAS-ActorVocabulary: The Seas Actor Vocabulary defined for the ITEA2 SEAS project
- SEAS-AreaOntology: This ontology is targeted for defining structure of buildings (or more general facilities) and zones related to control and measurement with links to various BIM (Building Information Model) related standards
- SEAS-BuildingCategoriesVocabulary: The SEAS Building Categories for the ITEA2 SEAS (Smart Energy Aware Systems) project. This module presents subcategories for classifying building related
- SEAS-EnergyFormVocabulary: This vocabulary defines forms of energy, such as ElectricEnergy, NuclearEnergy, MagneticEnergy or ThermalEnergy
- SEAS-ElectricityPlayerOntology: This ontology defines electricity players and electricity market, as systems that exchange electricity
- SEAS-ElectricPowerSystemVocabulary: The SEAS Electric Power System Vocabulary defines: (1) Electric power systems that consume, produce, or store electricity, (2) electrical connections between electric power systems, where electricity is exchanged, and (3) electrical connection Points of electric power systems, through which electricity flows in/out the power systems
- SEAS-FlexibilityVocabulary: The SEAS Flexibility Vocabulary defines code lists to interpret evaluations of operating features of interest. For instance, the value may be the minimal operating value
- SEAS-LightSystemOntology: This vocabulary defines light Systems, and their common properties

---

[3] http://www.mascem.gecad.isep.ipp.pt/ontologies/call-for-proposal.owl,   http://www.mascem.gecad. isep.ipp.pt/ontologies/electricity-markets-results.owl.

- SEAS-ThermodynamicSystemOntology: This ontology is targeted for defining thermodynamic systems and their relations
- SEAS-ThermodynamicSystemVocabulary: This vocabulary defines common properties of thermodynamic systems, and evaluation interpretation code lists

The developed ontologies not only enable the interoperability between different MAS but also represent the concepts needed to understand and use real data, from different sources. These data can be acquired in real time through analysers/sensors, or even databases available online. For that, the developed ontologies allow the representation of knowledge in a common vocabulary, regardless of the source; thus facilitating interoperability between the various heterogeneous systems and data, information and knowledge sources, with the ultimate goal of achieving an enhanced simulation platform for fully transactive energy systems.

4 Case Study

This case study intends to demonstrate the usefulness and advantage of using EMO to support players' participation in the market. The simulation scenario was created with the intention of representing the European reality through a summarized group of players, representing buyer and seller entities of each area of each regional market. It includes two agents (buyer and seller) per area, practicing the average prices and negotiating the total amount of power that have been transacted in each of these areas in the reality, for the day 16th January, 2013 (Wednesday).

Forty one areas are considered, i.e. 41 buyers and 41 sellers, resulting in a total of 82 players for this simulation. The selected market type is the symmetrical day-ahead pool without considering any complex offer or condition.

As the simulation starts, the market operator sends a call for proposal (CfP) to each registered player. Figure 2 presents a snippet of the CfP sent by the market operator. The full version can be found online[4].

Analyzing Fig. 2, it is possible to observe the definition of a *CallForProposal* (from line 40 to line 43) for the EM named *"MIBEL"* (defined from line 35 to 39).

After receiving the CfP, each player queries its knowledge base in order to send its proposal to the respective market operator. Figure 3 presents a snip of the *Proposal* sent by agent Seller 38. The complete version is available online[5].

Observing Fig. 3, it is noticeable the definition of an *Offer* for period 19 (between lines 572 and 578). The *Price* proposed for this offer is defined from line 567 to 571.

After receiving the proposals and validating all incoming offers, the market operator analyses the bids, and generates the RDF results to be sent to the participating players. An excerpt of the RDF result achieved by Seller 38 is illustrated in Fig. 4. The full version of this RDF can be found online[6], where the results may be observed with better insight.

---

[4] http://www.mascem.gecad.isep.ipp.pt/ontologies/paper/paams/16/CfP.rdf.

[5] http://www.mascem.gecad.isep.ipp.pt/ontologies/paper/paams/16/Proposal.rdf.

[6] http://www.mascem.gecad.isep.ipp.pt/ontologies/paper/paams/16/Result.rdf.

```
35    <rdf:Description rdf:about="mibel.owl#iM-MIBEL">
36        <emo:hasMarketType rdf:resource="mibel.owl#iMT-SPOT"/>
37        <emo:name>MIBEL</emo:name>
38        <rdf:type rdf:resource="mibel.owl#MIBEL"/>
39    </rdf:Description>
40    <rdf:Description rdf:about="call-for-proposal.owl#iCFP-DayAheadSession2013-01-16-0">
41        <cfp:forElectricityMarket rdf:resource="mibel.owl#iM-MIBEL"/>
42        <rdf:type rdf:resource="call-for-proposal.owl#CallForProposal"/>
43    </rdf:Description>
```

Fig. 2. CfP RDF snippet

```
567    <rdf:Description rdf:about="mibel.owl#iPrice1-P19-DayAheadSession2013-01-16-0">
568        <emo:value rdf:datatype="http://www.w3.org/2001/XMLSchema#double">60.04</emo:value>
569        <emo:unit>EUR</emo:unit>
570        <rdf:type rdf:resource="electricity-markets.owl#Price"/>
571    </rdf:Description>
572    <rdf:Description rdf:about="mibel.owl#iOffer1-P19-DayAheadSession2013-01-16-0">
573        <emo:hasPrice rdf:resource="mibel.owl#iPrice1-P19-DayAheadSession2013-01-16-0"/>
574        <emo:hasPower rdf:resource="mibel.owl#iPower1-P19-DayAheadSession2013-01-16-0"/>
575        <emo:number rdf:datatype="http://www.w3.org/2001/XMLSchema#unsignedInt">1</emo:number>
576        <emo:id rdf:datatype="http://www.w3.org/2001/XMLSchema#unsignedLong">3468251671864012524</emo:id>
577        <rdf:type rdf:resource="electricity-markets.owl#Offer"/>
578    </rdf:Description>
```

Fig. 3. Seller 38's proposal RDF snippet

```
67    <rdf:Description rdf:about="electricity-markets-results.owl#iTradedPower-HourlyResult-19">
68        <emo:unit>MW</emo:unit>
69        <emo:value rdf:datatype="http://www.w3.org/2001/XMLSchema#double">11364.2</emo:value>
70        <rdf:type rdf:resource="electricity-markets-results.owl#TradedPower"/>
71    </rdf:Description>
72    <rdf:Description rdf:about="electricity-markets-results.owl#iTradedPower-HourlyResult-8">
73        <emo:unit>MW</emo:unit>
74        <emo:value rdf:datatype="http://www.w3.org/2001/XMLSchema#double">11351.9</emo:value>
75        <rdf:type rdf:resource="electricity-markets-results.owl#TradedPower"/>
76    </rdf:Description>
77    <rdf:Description rdf:about="electricity-markets-results.owl#iMarketPrice-HourlyResult-19">
78        <emo:unit>EUR</emo:unit>
79        <emo:value rdf:datatype="http://www.w3.org/2001/XMLSchema#double">61.52</emo:value>
80        <rdf:type rdf:resource="electricity-markets-results.owl#MarketPrice"/>
81    </rdf:Description>
```

Fig. 4. Seller 38's result RDF snippet

By the analysis of Fig. 4 it is possible to observe the traded power of Seller 38 (between lines 67 and 71) and market clearing price (from line 77 to line 81) of period 19.

Figure 5 presents the results achieved by Seller 38 for each hourly period of the considered day. As it is possible to notice, Seller 38 sold almost all its available power for the 24 hourly periods of the day. In periods 4 and 6 Seller 38 was not able to sell any of the offered power. In turn, in period 5, this agent is the one who determines the market price, being only able to sell less than ¼ of its available power. Market prices vary approximately between €38 (period 4) and €75 (period 10).

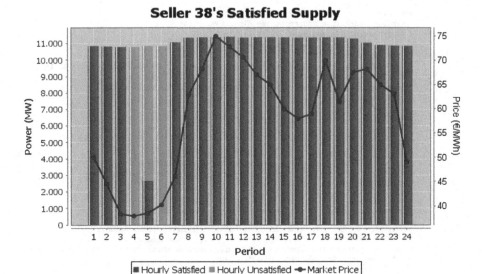

Fig. 5. Seller 38's satisfied supply

5 Conclusions

In order to disseminate the development of interoperable MAS within power engineering, interconnection issues must be addressed. To take full advantage of these systems, there is a growing need for knowledge exchange with the aim at providing full interoperability between different systems. With the objective of overcoming these issues, the *Electricity Markets Ontology* (EMO) is proposed, gathering the EM main concepts, enabling the interoperability of independent multi-agent based simulation platforms.

Additionally, particular modules conceived to deal with the different communications between power and energy players have also been developed. Using these ontologies, different types of agents are able to communicate with each other, understanding a common language, while providing the means for any agent from external systems to do the same, simply by importing the developed ontologies. By "speaking the same language", agents from different communities can understand each other and communicate efficiently, without the need for spending unnecessary computational resources and execution time (essential in a simulation process) in translating messages.

The developed ontology is publicly available online so it can be easily accessed, reused and extended by Ontology Engineers or MAS developers in the scope of EM. This is a relevant contribution, not only to provide the participation in joint simulations in the power and energy domain, but also to give the basis for the development of other systems specific ontologies. The comparison of the system's performance with and without the use of ontologies is considered as future work, as well as the conversion of RDF messages to JSON-LD[7] to reduce the computational weight of communications.

---

[7] http://json-ld.org/.

The presented case study has proven the usefulness and advantages of using the proposed ontologies in the scope of EM simulations. The new MAS society resulting from the integration of the proposed ontologies for interoperability of several MAS simulators, provides a solid platform to study and explore the implications and consequences of new and already existing approaches in EM. Researchers of the power systems area consider tools with this type of capabilities essential in order to be prepared to deal with the constant changes in the EM environment.

References

1. Sioshansi, F.P.: Evolution of Global Electricity Markets: New Paradigms, New Challenges, New Approaches (2013)
2. Ciarreta, A., Espinosa, M.P., Pizarro-Irizar, C.: Has renewable energy induced competitive behavior in the Spanish electricity market? Energy Policy **104**, 171–182 (2017)
3. Geng, Z., Conejo, A.J., Chen, Q., Xia, Q., Kang, C.: Electricity production scheduling under uncertainty: max social welfare vs. min emission vs. max renewable production. Appl. Energy **193**, 540–549 (2017)
4. Santos, G., Pinto, T., Praça, I., Vale, Z.: MASCEM: optimizing the performance of a multi-agent system. Energy **111**, 513–524 (2016)
5. Li, H., Tesfatsion, L.: Development of open source software for power market research: the AMES test bed. J. Energy Mark. **2**, 111–128 (2009)
6. Thimmapuram, P., Veselka, T.D., Koritarov, V., Vilela, S., Pereira, R., Silva, R.F.: Modeling hydro power plants in deregulated electricity markets: integration and application of EMCAS and VALORAGUA. In: 2008 5th International Conference on the European Electricity Market, EEM (2008)
7. Vale, Z., Pinto, T., Praça, I., Morais, H.: MASCEM: electricity markets simulation with strategic agents. IEEE Intell. Syst. **26**, 9–17 (2011)
8. Oliveira, P., Pinto, T., Morais, H., Vale, Z.: MASGriP a multi-agent smart grid simulation platform. In: IEEE Power and Energy Society General Meeting, pp. 1–8 (2012)
9. Pinto, T., Vale, Z., Sousa, T.M., Praça, I., Santos, G., Morais, H.: Adaptive learning in agents behaviour: a framework for electricity markets simulation. Integr. Comput. Aided Eng. **21**, 399–415 (2014)
10. Santos, G., Pinto, T., Vale, Z.: Ontologies for the interoperability of heterogeneous multi-agent systems in the scope of power and energy systems. In: De la Prieta, F., et al. (eds.) PAAMS 2017. AISC, vol. 619, pp. 300–301. Springer, Cham (2018). https://doi.org/10.1007/978-3-319-61578-3_42
11. Gomes, L., Faria, P., Morais, H., Vale, Z., Ramos, C.: Distributed, agent-based intelligent system for demand response program simulation in smart grids. IEEE Intell. Syst. **29**, 56–65 (2014)
12. Faia, R., Pinto, T., Abrishambaf, O., Fernandes, F., Vale, Z., Corchado, J.M.: Case based reasoning with expert system and swarm intelligence to determine energy reduction in buildings energy management. Energy Build. **155**, 269–281 (2017)
13. Teixeira, B., Pinto, T., Silva, F., Santos, G., Praça, I., Vale, Z.: Multi-agent decision support tool to enable interoperability among heterogeneous energy systems (2018)
14. Fernandes, F., Morais, H., Vale, Z., Ramos, C.: Dynamic load management in a smart home to participate in demand response events. Energy Build. **82**, 592–606 (2014). https://doi.org/10.1016/j.enbuild.2014.07.067

Modeling Herd Behavior Caused by Evacuation Decision Making Using Response Threshold

Akira Tsurushima[(✉)]

Intelligent Systems Laboratory, SECOM Co., Ltd., Mitaka, Tokyo, Japan
a-tsurushima@secom.co.jp

Abstract. Herd behavior is a cognitive bias in humans which is one of the causes of inappropriate or irrational behavior during evacuations. Although previous work in evacuation simulations have incorporated cognitive biases for realistic results, most of this work has focused on predefined rules or roles to implement these biases, leaving them unable to investigate the cause of herd behaviors. In this paper, an evacuation decision model based on the biological response threshold model is presented to reproduce human herd behaviors in evacuations. Since this model is independent of any predefined rules, it can be used for in-depth analysis of herding. Evacuation simulations using this model reveals that the uneven spatial distribution of evacuees causes an increase in the number of evacuees per unit time. It also shows that as the population density of the room increases, the number of evacuees per unit time increases rapidly.

1 Introduction

The influence of cognitive biases on human behaviors during disaster evacuations has attracted the attention of many researchers. It is widely recognized that the normalcy bias, the mental tendency to deny danger, was a major factor in the deaths of 196 passengers in the Daegu metro fire in Korea, February 2003 [13]. Herd behavior, which is caused by the mental tendency to decide one's behavior based on the behavior of others, has also been observed in many evacuations including the Three Mile Island nuclear power plant accident [4] and football stadium disasters in the United Kingdom [6]. Panic, which refers to inappropriate fear and flight, has also been reported in some accidents or disasters [6,10,14]. These inappropriate and irrational human behaviors sometimes result in serious loss of lives. Herding is one of the most representative and important behaviors among these behaviors.

Herding behavior in humans has been studied extensively in numerous fields and is also known as crowd behavior, conformity bias, peer effect, bandwagon effect and majority syncing bias [5,11,17]. In evolutionary psychology, herding is investigated as a form of social learning [11]. In ethology, the process of consensus decision making among individuals is studied [5]. In cognitive psychology, the

© Springer Nature Switzerland AG 2019
P. Davidsson and H. Verhagen (Eds.): MABS 2018, LNAI 11463, pp. 138–152, 2019.
https://doi.org/10.1007/978-3-030-22270-3_11

mechanisms of transition of thought and behavior are explored [17], and in social psychology, the social comparison processes are discussed [8].

In the field of multi-agent simulation, recent simulation models have started to take cognitive biases into account for more realistic simulation results. Iwanaga and Matsuura [12] analyzed the influence of normalcy bias and herd behavior on evacuation time in a tsunami evacuation simulation. Okaya et al. [15,16] studied how evacuation announcements and information transfer affect evacuation behaviors. Tsai et al. [19] developed an evacuation simulation model of Los Angeles international airport that embeds the herd behavior model based on social comparison theory [8]. Bulumulla et al. [3] incorporated the influence of the extra time required to assemble family or relatives spread over a large geographic area in their wildfire evacuation simulation. Foraqi and Mesgari [7] developed an emergency evacuation model that takes account of the influence of emotion.

However in all of these simulations, the agents have predefined rules or roles, such as the frequently used BDI (Belief-Desire-Intention) model [2], in which the researchers embedded the behaviors that they expected to appear [3,15,16, 19]. Although these built-in behaviors will occur within the simulation, they occur only under predefined conditions. Thus these models cannot be employed to analyze the mechanisms of why these behaviors arise in certain situations. Furthermore, it is neither possible to reproduce these behaviors under arbitrary conditions nor to explore the conditions under which these behaviors emerge.

Helbing et al. [9,10] developed the social force model that was originally used to represent pedestrian dynamics and was later extended to simulate panic behavior in evacuations. Without employing any predefined rules or roles, the model reproduced clogging or arch-like blocking in panic situations and also simulated the asymmetric use of two identical doors in one room. However, since Helbing's model consists of physical factors such as velocity, force, and friction, it is difficult to incorporate decisions or cognitive biases.

In this paper, an evacuation decision model is proposed that can reproduce human herd behaviors. The model represents the roles of decision making in evacuation situations and can naturally incorporate explicit decisions (e.g. choosing the closest door) or implicit cognitive biases (e.g. follow others) into agent behaviors. The model separates the influence of the decision making processes from physical behaviors, therefore allowing use in conjunction with physical behavior models like Helbing's model, possibly resulting in more realistic analysis of evacuations. NetLogo 5.0.2 [20] was used to develop the model and to conduct the experiments presented.

2   The Response Threshold Model

It is reasonable to assume that a herd consists of leaders and followers, where the leaders determine their behaviors through their own intentions and the followers determine their behaviors through the behavior of other leaders or followers, because if there is no leader, no one would be able to behave. However how to assign the roles of leader and follower to agents is unclear. This can be called the leader and follower problem.

Derek Sivers notes the importance of the first follower [18] in his famous talk at TED2010. He stated "the first follower is what transforms a lone nut into a leader," implying that leader and follower relationship is mutually dependent. In other words, leaders do not exist without any followers, and vice versa. The response threshold model [1] which is an ideal model to represent this kind of mutual relationship is adopted to solve the leader and follower problem.

The response threshold model is well known in biology and ecology as a model for division of labor in eusocial organisms. In the response threshold model, an individual in a colony has various response thresholds. The individual responds to task-related stimuli and engages in a task if a particular stimulus exceeds its response threshold. Since individuals with lower thresholds will respond to stimuli more sensitively, they will perform a task more frequently than those who have higher thresholds. Successful task performance suppresses the intensity of the task related stimuli.

In the simplified response threshold model discussed above, a task to be performed and it is associated with a stimulus s. The intensity of the stimulus will increase if it is not performed sufficiently because of an insufficient number of individuals to engage in the task. An individual i has a random variable X representing its mental state and a response threshold θ_i. The individual is active (engaging in the task) if $X = 1$, and inactive (not engaging in the task) if $X = 0$. The probability P_i that an individual will be active per unit time is:

$$P_i(X = 0 \to X = 1) = \frac{s^2}{s^2 + \theta_i^2}. \tag{1}$$

The probability ϵ that an individual gives up task performance and is inactive is constant:

$$P_i(X = 1 \to X = 0) = \epsilon. \tag{2}$$

The intensity of the task associated stimulus per unit time is given by:

$$s(t + 1) = s(t) + \delta - \alpha \frac{c}{C} \tag{3}$$

where δ is the increase of the stimulus per unit time, α is a scale factor measuring the efficiency of task performance, c is the number of individuals currently engaging in the task, and C is the total number of individuals in the colony.

To apply this model to the leader and follower problem, the task to be performed is to remove all agents from the room. An agent has two mental states, a leader ($X = 1$) or a follower ($X = 0$). C is the number of agents initially in the room and c is the number of agents who have exited the room at the moment Eq. (3) is evaluated. However, both C and c are require global information that each agent may not know. Instead of using global information, each agent i can use a local estimation ρ_i for task performance. Thus Eq. (3) becomes:

$$s_i(t + 1) = s_i(t) + \delta - \alpha \rho_i. \tag{4}$$

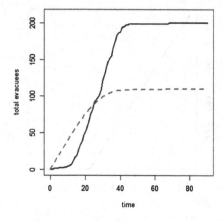

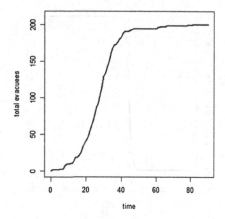

Fig. 1. Cumulative number of evacuees with a global stimulus s. The black solid line indicates the number of evacuees and the red dashed line shows the value of s. (Color figure online)

Fig. 2. Cumulative number of evacuees in the simulation with local stimuli s_i.

Each agent has its own stimulus s_i in Eq. (4), whereas all agents share the same stimulus s in Eq. (3).

Consider the local estimation ρ_i of the task performance in the leader and follower problem. Since the task is to have all agents leave the room, the number of agents in an agent's vicinity could be used as ρ_i. Thus,

$$\rho_i = 1 - \frac{n}{N_{max}} \tag{5}$$

where N_{max} is the maximum number of agents in the vicinity of the agent, and n is the number of agents in the vicinity of the agent at the moment.

Figures 1 and 2 show examples of the simulation of the leader and follower problem using the response threshold model. Figure 1 is the case with the global stimulus s, the black solid line shows the cumulative number of agents who left the room, and the red dashed line shows the value of s. Figure 2 is the case with the local estimate s_i of the stimulus s, the black solid line shows the cumulative number of agents who left the room. The task is successfully performed in both cases, and the local estimates of the stimulus works well, since the black solid lines in two charts in Figs. 1 and 2 are almost identical.

3   The Evacuation Decision Model

A model that represents human herd behaviors in evacuations can be developed by extending the model presented in Sect. 2. Since the risk perception of individual will vary, a parameter μ is introduced which represents an individual's risk sensitivity. The agent's behaviors may not be necessarily consistent with the risk perception μ, because behaviors are also affected by surrounding agents.

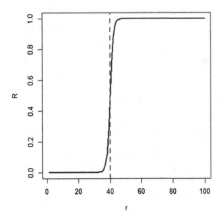
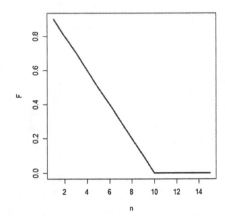

Fig. 3. The risk cognition function assuming $g = 0.5$ and $\mu = 40$.

Fig. 4. The task progress function assuming $N_{max} = 10$.

Assume the environment has an risk value r which expresses the level of objective risks in the environment. An agent with μ_i will respond to the situation by the function:

$$R(r) = \frac{1}{1 + e^{-g(r - \mu_i)}} \qquad (6)$$

where g is the activation gain which determines the slope of the sigmoid function (Fig. 3). All agents share the same risk value r, but each agent will respond differently since μ_i is agent specific.

In this model, the stimulus of the agent i is defined as:

$$s_i(t + 1) = max\{s_i(t) + \hat{\delta} - \alpha(1 - R)F, \ 0\} \qquad (7)$$

where $\hat{\delta}$ is the increase of the stimulus per unit time

$$\hat{\delta} = \begin{cases} \delta & \text{if } r > 0 \\ 0 & \text{otherwise,} \end{cases} \qquad (8)$$

α is a scale factor of the stimulus, R is the risk perception function given by Eq. (6), and F is the task progress function:

$$F(n) = \begin{cases} 1 - n/N_{max} & n < N_{max} \\ 0 & \text{otherwise,} \end{cases} \qquad (9)$$

where n is the number of agents in the vicinity, and N_{max} is the maximum number of agents in the vicinity (Fig. 4). Since the first term of max in Eq. (7) only becomes negative when the task is already performed sufficiently, activation of the agent with a negative stimulus due to Eq. (1) is unnecessary. Thus Eq. (7) only takes non-negative values.

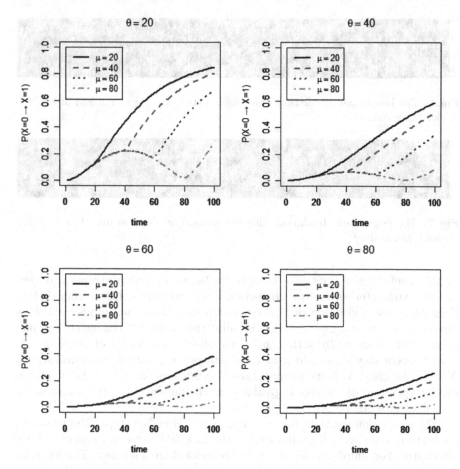

Fig. 5. The shapes of the probability $P(X = 0 \rightarrow X = 1)$ for $\theta = 20, 40, 60, 80$ and $\mu = 20, 40, 60, 80$ assuming $\delta = 0.5$, $\alpha = 1.2$, $N_{max} = 10$, and $g = 1.0$.

Figure 5 shows the shapes of the probability $P(X = 0 \rightarrow X = 1)$ when θ and μ take several different values. The value of r starts from 0 and linearly increases to 100, and the value of n starts from 10 and decreases linearly to 0 in 100 time units. These charts shows that a lower θ_i or a lower μ_i always results in a higher probability of being active $(X = 1)$, and the probability always increases whenever the value of r exceeds μ_i.

4   The Evacuation Simulation

4.1   Setup

A rectangular room (16 × 128 grids) is filled with 600 randomly distributed agents, and the room has a risk value r that expresses the level of some threats against the agents in the room. The only exit is located at the left end of the

Fig. 6. The benchmark simulation which agents start moving at random at $t = 120$. (Color figure online)

Fig. 7. The evacuation simulation with the evacuation decision model at $t = 120$. (Color figure online)

room, therefore the agents must move to the left to evacuate the room. An agent has two parameters θ_i and μ_i whose values are arbitrarily chosen from $(0, 100]$. Each agent has a visibility of 120 degrees with a distance of 5 grids toward the direction to the exit. This visibility is called the vicinity of the agent, and only agents that are currently within this range affect the behavior of the agent.

The agent moves one grid toward the exit per unit time if its mental state is $X = 1$. The agent with the mental state $X = 0$ moves one grid if the number of moving agents in its vicinity is greater than the number of stopped agents, but does not move otherwise.

The simulation starts from 0 and terminates after 360 steps. The value of r increases linearly from 0 to 100 during the first 200 steps and remains at 100 afterwards. For simplicity, all agents in the room share a single r. The following values are assumed: $\epsilon = 0.2$, $\delta = 0.5$, $\alpha = 1.2$, $N_{max} = 10$, and $g = 1.0$.

The simulation focuses only on the psychological aspect of agents, ignoring the physical factors such as collisions, clogging, and disturbances.

4.2 Results and Analysis

For comparison with the evacuation decision model, first a benchmark simulation is conducted where agents start moving at random. Figure 6 shows a screen capture of the benchmark in which an agent starts evacuating whenever r exceeds μ_i. Since μ_i is randomly distributed, agents start moving at random. Green agents have started moving and yellow agents are not yet moving.

Figure 7 shows a screen capture of the simulation in which the evacuation decision model, described in Sect. 3, is incorporated into the agents. The agents with mental state $X = 1$ are indicated in red and the agents with mental state $X = 0$ are indicated in green or yellow; green agents are currently moving and yellow agents are not yet moving.

Both Figs. 6 and 7 were taken 120 steps after the simulations was started. In Fig. 6, all agents are evenly distributed over the room regardless of their colors.

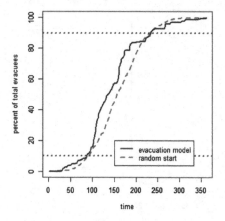

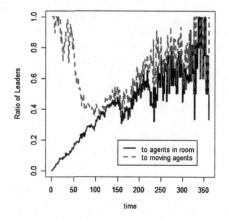

Fig. 8. Cumulative number of evacuees in random start (red) and the evacuation decision model (black). (Color figure online)

Fig. 9. The ratio of leaders in the evacuation decision model. (Color figure online)

In contrast, in Fig. 7, agents are unevenly distributed and the only yellow agents left are in the farthest region from the exit. This is because the agents in the farther region have fewer chances of being affected by others since all agents move in the same direction.

Figure 8 shows the percentage of the total number of evacuees during the simulation. The red dashed line indicates the percentage of evacuees when the agents start evacuating at random (Fig. 6) and the black solid line indicates the percentage when the agents are equipped with the evacuation decision model (Fig. 7). The ratio of the leaders in the black solid line in Fig. 8 is given in Fig. 9. The black solid line in Fig. 9 shows the ratio of leaders to the number of agents still in the room, and the red dashed line indicates the ratio of leaders to the number of agents who are moving at that moment. The red dashed line in Fig. 9 shows that all moving agents are leaders at the beginning of the simulation, then many followers appear leading to a decrease in the ratio of the leaders, with a gradual increase in the ratio until the end of the simulation. These two lines eventually overlap, because all agents in the room are moving at the end of the simulation.

Agent vicinity is an important factor in herd behavior. In the original simulation, the range was set to five grids. The effect of varying the radius of the vicinity from two to 20 grids is shown in Fig. 10. The Y-axis represents the variance in the times that each agent starts moving. It can be seen in Fig. 10 that if the vicinity of an agent is small, the variance of the starting times is large, while if the vicinity is larger, the variance will decrease. If the vicinity is set to zero, the agent is unaffected by other agents, thus all agents will behave individually and herd behavior will not occur. If the range is large enough to cover all other agents, almost all agents will behave simultaneously, because every agent will affect each other.

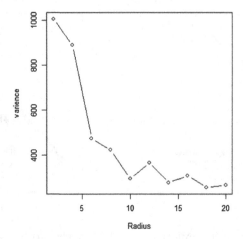

Fig. 10. The radius of the vicinity and the variance in the agent start times

4.3   Impact of Uneven Spatial Distributions

The main contribution of the evacuation decision model is the spatial patterns of unevenly distributed agents during evacuation given in Fig. 7. However, the effect of these uneven spatial distributions in real evacuations is still unclear.

An investigation of the relation between evacuation time and population density using the evacuation decision model reveals that the evacuation times are clearly affected by the model. The evacuation times required for 10% and 90% of the agents complete their evacuations (the blue dotted lines in Fig. 8) were adopted as indices to indicate the total evacuations. Simulations were conducted 20 times each, with a varying number of agents (200, 400, 600, 800, and 1000). As a benchmark, simulations with random starts were conducted[1] (Fig. 6) and compared to the evacuation times of the evacuation decision model.

The results are shown in Fig. 11. Upper items show the times that 90% of the agents complete evacuations and lower items show the times that 10% of the agents complete evacuations. The leftmost items show the benchmarks that all agents start evacuating at random, and followed by the cases of 200, 400, 600, 800, and 1000 agents with the evacuation decision model.

Comparing the benchmarks results with the simulation results, it clearly shows that the evacuation completion times are affected by the evacuation decision model. Moreover, the results of the evacuation decision model indicate that the population density of the room has a great deal of influence on evacuation completion time. Overall, as the population density increases, the evacuation completion time tends to decrease. With 200 agents, the evacuation completion time is slower than the benchmark. However, in the case of 1000 agents, the 90% evacuation completion time has been shortened to about 150 units, much shorter

---

[1] The evacuation times were unchanged regardless of the number of agents in the case of random start.

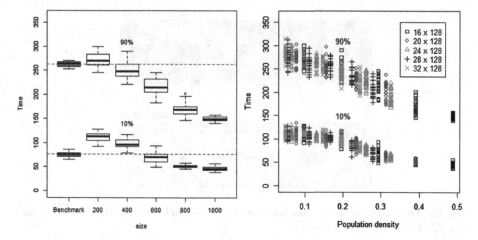

Fig. 11. The evacuation completion times of the simulations with 200, 400, 600, 800, and 1000 agents. The left-most items (indicated in red) show the random start benchmarks. Upper and lower items show 90% and 10% evacuation completion times, respectively. (Color figure online)

Fig. 12. Population density and evacuation completion time. The different colors show the different sizes of the room. (Color figure online)

than that of the benchmark which is about 270 units. The time between 90% and 10% evacuation completion time shows the time that is required to evacuate 80% of agents. In the benchmark, 80% of agents evacuate in about 200 units, yet the evacuation times of 80% agents are much smaller in the cases with the evacuation decision model. In comparison with the number of agents actually evacuated, 160 agents evacuated in 157 time units in the case with 200 agents, whereas 800 agents evacuated in 103 time units in the case of 1000 agents. While the population density increased by a factor of five, the number of evacuees per unit time has increased by a factor of 7.62.

All of the above simulations were conducted by assuming a room with 16×128 grids which was somewhat narrow and long. Simulations were also conducted by varying the width of the room to 20, 24, 28, and 32 grids. In these settings, the areas of the room are $1.25, 1.50, 1.75$, and 2.00 times as large as the original setting. By comparing the number of agents per grid, the effect of population density can be examined.

The results with different rooms sizes are shown in Fig. 12. The figure shows both 10% and 90% evacuation completion times are shortened as the population density of the room increases, and the distance between the two walls are also decreased. The variance of the results becomes smaller as the population density increases. These result show that the evacuation times are affected by the population densities regardless of the sizes and shapes of the room.

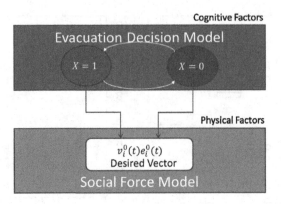

Fig. 13. The output of the evacuation decision model can be used as the desired vector $v_i^0(t)e_i^0(t)$ in the social force model.

5   Cognitive Aggregation and Physical Factors

The evacuation decision model presented in this paper only deals with cognitive or psychological factors such as decision making and cognitive bias; physical factors such as collisions, clogging, and disturbances are not considered at all. Therefore, an agent can simply pass through other agents, even though they are positioned in front of it. Nonetheless, the evacuation decision model shows that various types of congestion occur in evacuation situations. Since these types of congestion occur purely due to cognitive factors, we label them as cognitive aggregation.

The evacuation simulation (Sect. 4) reproduced the uneven spatial distribution of evacuees and showed that as population density increases, these uneven distribution will cause an increase in the number of evacuees per unit time, eventually leading to physical congestion. It is worth noting that the cognitive aggregation occurred despite disregarding physical factors. In Sect. 4.3, 103 time units were required for 800 agents to evacuate without regard to physical factors. The effect of incorporating physical factors into the model is likely to affect the evacuation time.

To model this behavior, the social force model [9] can be employed in conjunction with the evacuation simulation model (Fig. 13), since the evacuation decision model itself is simple.

The social force model is given as

$$m_i \frac{d\boldsymbol{v}_i}{dt} = m_i \frac{v_i^0(t)e_i^0(t) - \boldsymbol{v}_i(t)}{\tau_i} + \sum_{j(\neq i)} \boldsymbol{f}_{ij} + \sum_W \boldsymbol{f}_{iW} \qquad (10)$$

where m_i is the mass of an agent i, $d\boldsymbol{v}_i/dt$ is the change of velocity at time t, v_i^0 is the desired speed, e_i^0 is the desired direction, $\boldsymbol{f}_{ij}$ is the interaction force between the agent i and the agent j, and $\boldsymbol{f}_{iW}$ is the interaction force between agent i and the walls. The output of the evacuation decision model can be used as the desired vector $v_i^0(t)e_i^0(t)$ in the social force model (Fig. 13). By doing this, the social force model can take physical factors[2] into account and prevent agents from passing through others.

In the case of the evacuation decision model with the social force model (EDM+SFM), the overall behavior is very similar to the one in the simple evacuation decision model (EDM). Uneven spatial distributions are also observed in EDM+SFM. However, the behavior of each agent is slightly different, such as agents frequently changing directions to avoid others until some spatial patterns are to be formed.

6 Population and Physical Factors

The same simulations as in Sect. 4.3 are conducted to investigate the relation between the evacuation completion times and population in EDM+SFM. The results are given in Fig. 14.

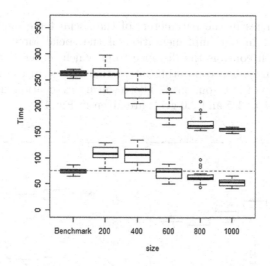

Fig. 14. The evacuation completion times in EDM+SFM.

Figure 14 is similar to the results of EDM in Fig. 11. To further examine these results, the median evacuation completion times for each simulation are shown in Table 1. In this table, the median time to evacuate 800 agents are is shown in the columns labeled "Difference." For the highest population size of 1000 agents, evacuations of 800 agents require 102.5 time units when physical

---

[2] The factors associated with the social force model are not purely physical. Psychological tendencies of two pedistrians to stay away from each other are incorporated. However, the original causes of such factors are the physical existence of walls or others, thus we call them physical factors.

factors are incorporated (EDM+SFM), whereas if physical factors are ignored (simple EDM), 103.0 time units are required. The evacuation completion times are nearly unchanged regardless of whether physical factors are incorporated.

Table 1. The median of the evacuation completion time for the first 10% and 90% of agents and their differences in each population size for EDM and EDM+SFM cases.

Population	EDM			EDM+SFM		
	10% time	90% time	Difference	10% time	90% time	Difference
200	113.5	270.5	157.0	108.5	260.0	151.5
400	95.5	248.5	153.0	106.5	232.0	125.5
600	69.5	215.0	145.5	74.0	188.0	114.0
800	51.0	168.0	117.0	61.0	162.0	101.0
1000	45.5	148.5	103.0	53.5	156.0	102.5

However, changes in the parameters of the social force model can greatly affect the results. In our implementation of the social force model, there is a parameter which controls the distance from which an agent will take other agents into account when computing interaction forces. In the case of Fig. 14, this parameter was set to one grid. The resulting evacuation times when this parameter was set to 1.5 and 2.0 grids are given in Fig. 15.

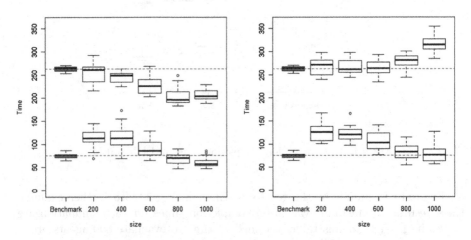

Fig. 15. The left and right charts are the results when the distance parameter was set to 1.5 and 2.0 grids, respectively.

Compare Fig. 14 with the right chart in Fig. 15. The time required to evacuate 80% of agents is 238.5 time units when this parameter is 2.0 grids (the right chart in Fig. 15), while it is 102.5 time units when this parameter is 1.0 grids (Fig. 14). These show that as the population density becomes greater, physical factors have greater impact on evacuation completion times.

7   Discussion

As discussed in Sect. 6, the evacuation completion times varies according to the distance parameter of the social force model.

The value of this parameter will depend on the situation that the simulation is modeling. In imminent dangerous situations and other similar situations were people rush to the exit without regard to distances between each other, this parameter should be set to a small value. In this case, the evacuation completion times will become short and the times from EDM and EDM+SFM will be similar. This is exactly the case shown in Fig. 14 which is almost identical to Fig. 11. This implies that as a situation becomes more serious, cognitive aggregation will be more important than physical factors.

Understanding cognitive aggregation is vital, especially for the spatial design of buildings, halls, stadiums, and other structures. If the architect ignores the effect of cognitive aggregation and considers only the physical factors, it is feasible that unexpected accidents occur during an evacuation.

Furthermore, the evacuation decision model also hints at the causes of cognitive aggregation. The evacuation simulation has shown that the population density of the space and the agent vicinity size have a large impact on the occurrence of congestion. By taking this factor into account, efficient designs for evacuation that avoid cognitive aggregation may be possible.

8   Conclusion

In this paper, an evacuation decision model which reproduces human herd behaviors in disaster evacuation situations was presented. The model represents cognitive bias of the agents, and was developed on the basis of the response threshold model in biology. Without employing any predefined rules, the evacuation simulation with the evacuation decision model have showed the occurrence of uneven spatial distribution of the evacuees that will cause an increase of the number of evacuees per unit time as population density increase. In order to take physical factors into account, the social force model can easily be employed in conjunction with the evacuation decison model.

Acknowledgements. The author is grateful to Yoshikazu Shinoda and Kei Marukawa for their helpful comments and suggestions.

References

1. Bonabeau, E., Theraulaz, G., Deneubourg, J.L.: Quantitative study of the fixed threshold model for the regulation of division of labour in insect societies. Proc. R. Soc. B **263**(1376), 1565–1569 (1996)

2. Bratman, M.: Intention, Plans, and Practical Reason. Harvard University Press, Cambridge (1987)
3. Bulumulla, C., Padgham, L., Singh, D., Chan, J.: The importance of modeling realistic human behaviour when planning evacuation schedules. In: Proceedings of the 16th International Conference on Autonomous Agents and Multiagent Systems, AAMAS 2017, pp. 446–454 (2017)
4. Cutter, S., Barnes, K.: Evacuation behavior and Three Mile Island. Disasters **6**(2), 116–124 (1982)
5. Dyer, J.R.G., et al.: Consensus decision making in human crowds. Anim. Behav. **75**, 461–470 (2008)
6. Elliott, D., Smith, D.: Football stadia disasters in the United Kingdom: learning from tragedy? Ind. Environ. Crisis Q. **7**(3), 205–229 (1993)
7. Faroqi, H., Mesgari, M.S.: Agent-based crowd simulation considering emotion contagion for emergency evacuation problem. In: International Conference on Sensors and Models in Remote Sensing and Photogrammetry, pp. 193–196 (2015)
8. Festinger, L.: A theory of social comparison processes. Hum. Relat. **7**(2), 117–140 (1954)
9. Helbing, D., Farkas, I., Vicsek, T.: Simulating dynamical features of escape panic. Nature **407**(28), 487–490 (2000). http://angel.elte.hu/panic/
10. Helbing, D., Farkas, I.J., Molnar, P., Vicsek, T.: Simulation of pedestrian crowds in normal and evacuation situations. Pedestr. Evacuation Dyn. **21**(2), 21–58 (2002)
11. Henrich, J., Boyd, R.: The evolution of conformist transmission and the emergence of between-group differences. Evol. Hum. Behav. **19**, 215–241 (1998)
12. Iwanaga, S., Matsuura, Y.: Considering psychological conditions in a Tsunami evacuation simulation. Commun. Comput. Inf. Sci. **442**, 437–446 (2014)
13. Marlair, G., Le Coze, J.C., Woon-Hyung, K., Galea, E.R.: Human behavior as a key factor in tunnel fire safety issues. In: Asia-Oceania Symposium on Fire Science & Technology, pp. 658–668 (2004)
14. Mawson, A.R.: Understanding mass panic and other collective responses to threat and disaster. Psychiatry **68**(2), 95–113 (2005)
15. Okaya, M., Niwa, T., Takahashi, T.: TENDENKO: agent-based evacuation drill and emergency planning system. In: Proceedings of the 13th International Conference on Autonomous Agents and Multiagent Systems, AAMAS 2014, pp. 1669–1670 (2014)
16. Okaya, M., Southern, M., Takahashi, T.: Dynamic information transfer and sharing model in agent based evacuation simulations. In: Proceedings of 12th International Conference on Autonomous Agents and Multiagent Systems, AAMAS 2013, pp. 1295–1296 (2013)
17. Raafat, R.M., Chater, N., Frith, C.: Herding in humans. Trends Cogn. Sci. **13**(10), 420–428 (2009)
18. Sivers, D.: How to start a movement. In: TED 2010 (2010). https://www.ted.com/talks/derek_sivers_how_to_start_a_movement
19. Tsai, J., et al.: ESCAPES - evacuation simulation with children, authorities, parents, emotions, and social comparison. In: Proceedings of 10th International Conference on Autonomous Agents and Multiagent Systems, AAMAS 2011, pp. 457–464 (2011)
20. Wilensky, U.: NetLogo (1999). http://ccl.northwestern.edu/netlogo/. Center for Connected Learning and Computer-Based Modeling, Northwestern University, Evanston, IL

Author Index

Printed in the United States
By Bookmasters